THE
ALL-AGE
SERVICE
ANNUAL

Volume Three

15 Bible-based service outlines for those who plan or lead all-age worship

52 sets of 'starter' activities for all ages, linked with the *Light* curriculum, for use at the start or end of a service

ISBN 978 1 84427 381 2

Scripture Union, 207–209 Queensway, Bletchley, MK2 2EB, England.
Email: info@scriptureunion.org.uk
Website: www.scriptureunion.org.uk

Scripture Union Australia
Locked Bag 2, Central coast Business Centre, NSW 2252, Australia
Website: www.scriptureunion.org.au

Scripture Union USA,
PO Box 987, Valley Forge, PA 19482, USA
Website: www.scriptureunion.org

All the *Learn and remember* verses are taken from the Contemporary English Version © American Bible Society 1991,1992,1995, Anglicisations © British and Foreign Bible Society 1997, or from the Good News Bible © American Bible Society 1992, both published in the UK by by HarperCollins*Publishers*. Used by permission.

Other Scripture quotations are taken from the New International Version © International Bible Society, Anglicisations © 2001, used by permissio of Hodder and Stoughton Ltd.

British Library Cataloguing-in-Publication Data
A catalogue record for this book is available from the British Library.

Printed by Tien Wah Press, Malaysia
Cover design Kevin Wade
Internal layout Helen Jones

Scripture Union is an international Christian charity working with churches in more than 130 countries, providing resources to bring the good news about Jesus to children, young people and families and encourage them to develop spiritually through the Bible and prayer.

As well as our network of volunteers, staff and associates who run holidays, church-based events and school Christian groups, we produce a wide range of publications and support those who use our resources through training programmes.

CONTENTS

How the All-Age Service Annual works

This resource takes the stress out of planning and leading all-age services and, if you are a user of Scripture Union's *Light* material, enables everyone to be discovering the same things about God when they are together and in their own sessions.

Part One

In many churches, children and adults share worship times together at the beginning or the end of the service. Service leaders and children's workers frequently comment on what a challenge it is to offer genuine and relevant all-age content for this part of the service. This book offers 52 sets of four activities to use in the academic year 2009–2010. But the activities in themselves are a rich toolbox for anyone looking for ideas to use in all-age worship. The starters are also available online, along with additional downloadable material – see www.scriptureunion.org.uk/light. Each set draws on the theme of one *Light* session, introducing or reinforcing what has been suggested in the children's or young people's material.

Part Two

15 creative service outlines are provided to be used throughout the year. Twelve of them take the Bible material of a Scripture Union *Light* curriculum series for the academic year 2009–2010, and develop a service around it. This means that if you have a monthly all-age service, the theme of that service will tie in with, broaden or reinforce what the children have been learning in their groups. A different but complementary Bible passage has been used, so there will not be any duplication. (Of course, the outlines can be used quite independently of the *Light* programme.) There are also three seasonal service outlines – a nativity service, Mothering Sunday and harvest. There is additional downloadable material available on the *Light* website: www.scriptureunion.org.uk/light, along with other all-age service outlines for festival occasions.

Other Scripture Union all-age resources :

Light for the Lectionary

Light for the Lectionary is published quarterly. It contains 15 flexible all-age service outlines that develop Bible passages and themes from *Common Worship* or the *Revised Common Lectionary*. It includes plenty of ideas that can be used throughout the year and is also a valuable resource for those who do not use a lectionary. For more details visit www.scriptureunion.org.uk/light.

Top Tips on All-age Worship

This is a 32-page book full of practical pointers on working with children and young people. Reading this would encourage you to reflect on and evaluate your all-age services. Other particularly useful Top Tips titles are *Growing Faith with Families* and *Encouraging Faith to Grow*.

The All-Age Service Annual Volume Three has been developed in direct response to what service leaders have told us about their services and needs. Our hope is that as you use these starters and outlines you will be able to lead your church family to encounter the living God together. No one ever said that leading all-age worship is easy but effective all-age services will have an impact into eternity:

- children and young people are respected and valued, so they are more likely to be committed to belonging to the body of Christ
- a spirit of inclusivity where people of all ages and abilities worship and learn together is far more welcoming to the visitor or outsider
- God's people put into practice the belief that generations need each other in the world that God made. We communicate this to a society where contact across the generations is often fragile.

Ro Willoughby

Ro Willoughby
Editor

We would like to thank the following for their writing contributions:

Starters: Marjory Francis, Christine Wright, Maggie Barfield, Victoria Beech.

Service outlines: Rachel Taylor, Rona Orme, Andrew Evans, Lizzie Green, Nick Harding, Eric Leese, 'Tricia Williams, John Grayston, Ali Walton, Amy Robinson, Malc' Halliday, Sera Rumble, Sarah Bingham.

PART ONE

All-age service starters

In many churches, people of all ages come together, either just for the beginning or for the end of the service. The reasons for this are varied but include the convenience for parents in collecting their children, or enabling children and young people to experience something of what it means to be in an adult church. But far more than this, it is a regular opportunity for everyone to live out what it means to be a valued member of God's family, worshipping, sharing and learning together, one among a crowd. Getting the timing right is a challenge, for which there is no easy answer! Finding appropriate activities for this part of the service can also be a challenge, which is why the All-age starters are a new feature in *The All-Age Service Annual Volume Three*.

Many churches would want adults and children to explore the same themes in their separate groups. These starters go some way towards making that possible, by enabling everyone to encounter the theme of the younger church members' *Light* session during the time when everyone is all together.

This part of the book can be used as follows:
- as a rich toolbox of ideas to use anytime when all ages are together in church
- to provide four activities that make a clear link to the material that is being used in any one session in the *Light* curriculum of 2009–2010, either before or after children leave
- to complement the service outlines in Part 2 of this book, with additional material on a series theme (Each set of starters contains theme introduction, suggested songs, prayer activity and an extra idea.)
- each *Light* series theme has a Learn and remember verse which is printed at the beginning of each series of starters. (These could become a feature of your services throughout the year, as everyone seeks to learn and remember God's Word in their heart!)

These starters are also available on the website, as is additional downloadable material, all to be found on www.scriptureunion.org.uk/light – All-Age Service Annual Volume Three. The downloads are numbered in order of appearance: for example, **web ref AASA3.starters_1 or 2**.

Each set of starters is linked to a series in *Light* for 2009–2010 and is therefore designed for a specific month. But it is recognised that many churches run their *Light* sessions in months other than the one specified.

Songs from the following songbooks and CDs are suggested. Of course, songs are found in more than one songbook and it would be impossible to refer to every songbook! The following books and CDs are referred to, with their abbreviations in brackets.

Songs of Fellowship (Books 1–4), Kingsway Music (*SOF*)
kids source, Kevin Mayhew Ltd, 1999 (*ks*)
kids source 2, world wide worship, 2002 (*ks2*)
the source, Kevin Mayhew Ltd, 1998 (*ts*)
Mission Praise, Marshall Pickering, 1990 (*MP*)
Junior Praise, Marshall Pickering, 1999 (*JP*)
Carol Praise, HarperCollinsPublishers, 2006 (*CP*)
Great Big God CD (*GBG*)
Light for everyone CD, Scripture Union, 2005 (*LFE*)
Bitesize Bible Songs CD, Scripture Union, 2007 (*BSBS*)
Bitesize Bible Songs 2 CD, Scripture Union, 2008 (*BSBS2*)
Reach Up! CD, Scripture Union, 2005 (*RU*)
Big Bible Storybook CD, Scripture Union, 2008 (*BBS*)

All the Scripture Union songs can be purchased on the appropriate CD from Scripture Union Mail Order, from the website or from all good Christian bookshops. However, the songs can also be purchased as downloads from www.scriptureunion.org.uk/light.

The audio recordings of the stories from the *Big Bible Storybook* (SU) can be bought on *The Big Bible Storybook* CD (SU) but can also be individually downloaded free from www.scriptureunion.org.uk/light, under All-Age Service Annual Volume Three, **web ref AASA3. starters_1.** *The Big Bible Storybook* is especially helpful in making an all-age service suitable for under-fives.

Jesus our Saviour

This series gives an opportunity to take time to explore the story of the death and resurrection of Jesus, in the detail and depth that is not always possible at other times of the year.

> **Learn and remember verse:**
> **'For God loved the world so much that he gave his only Son, so that everyone who believes in him may not die but have eternal life.' John 3:16**

The song 'So much', from *Bitesize Bible Songs 2*, puts these words to music and can be downloaded from www.scriptureunion.org.uk/light.

The all-age service outline that is part of this series is 'Spectators at the cross' on page 62, focusing on Psalm 22:1–8,14–18; Mark 15:24–30,33–47.

Oct – Dec
1

Jesus' last meal

Bible passage: Matthew 26:17–35
Session aim: To listen to Jesus as he tells his friends he is going to die

Theme introduction

Ask three or four people to deliver part of a speech given at a meal. The congregation will be asked to guess the occasion of the meal. Those giving the 'speech' should be careful to keep the occasion secret. The occasions could be: a wedding ('We wish Wally and Molly all the best for their future together.'); a birthday party ('Now blow out the candles on the cake.'); a school dinner ('Anyone for second helpings of mince? No? Well, pass the plates along.'); the Lord Mayor's Banquet ('Your Majesty, Prime Minister, my Lords, Ladies and Gentlemen, welcome to this ancient hall.')

After the quiz, say that speeches are often made at mealtimes. Sometimes we remember the occasion and the speech for ever, as is true of the meal and speech the children will hear about today, Jesus' last supper. If it is your custom to include children in a service of Holy Communion, it would be especially appropriate to hold such a service this session.

Song suggestions

'Broken for me, broken for you'	*SOF 53*
'Come let us sing of a wonderful love'	*SOF 72*
'I am the bread of life'	*SOF 200*
'Let us break bread together'	*SOF 330*
'So much'	*BBS2*

Prayer idea

The prayer below focuses on listening to some of Jesus' words and praying personally around them. Read this slowly, allowing plenty of time for pauses.

Jesus said to Judas, 'You will betray me.' Jesus said to Peter, 'You will deny me.'
Lord Jesus, it isn't only your enemies who betray or deny you. Sometimes your friends do too. Forgive me for the times I have let you down. Thank you for the way you have taken me back, time after time. Help me to be faithful to you. *(Pause.)*

Jesus gave thanks for the bread and broke it. He said, 'This is my body.' He took a cup of wine and said, 'This is my blood to be poured out.'
Lord Jesus, thank you for giving your body and shedding your blood for me. Thank you for the great love you have for me, love that will never stop loving. *(Pause.)*

Jesus said, 'I will not eat another Passover meal until it is finally eaten in God's kingdom.'
Lord Jesus, thank you for the hope your death brings to me – the forgiveness of my sin and the joy of life with you for ever. *(Pause.)*

Extra idea

Read Matthew 26:17–30 in a dramatised form with a group or use the Dramatised Bible.

You could listen to this story from *The Big Bible Storybook* audio book, 'A meal with Jesus'.

Jesus is arrested

Bible passage: Matthew 26:36–56
Session aim: To recognise that Jesus willingly chose to die

Theme introduction

Ask everybody to think about the choices they might make if their plane crashed in the African wilderness and they were the only survivor. .What would they choose to do in these situations?

A river must be crossed. Would you
* walk over a bridge that has a lion standing at the end
* swim through crocodile-infested waters?

The only food available is some slimy, creepy-crawly insects. Would you
* eat them
* starve yourself, hoping someone would rescue you soon?

Would you sleep
* up a tree (out of the way of lions but perhaps in reach of leopards)
* in a cave (out of sight but with no way of escape if a wild animal came inside)?

Either discuss the options in small groups, or people could raise their hands or move to a designated area depending on which choices they make – for example, to the left for 'Choice A' and the right for 'Choice B'.

Point out that these were very difficult choices and, in each case, a matter of life or death. Explain that Jesus had a life-or-death choice to make. What did he choose and why? The children will be thinking about this later.

Song suggestions

'I will offer up my life'	SOF 851
'It is a thing most wonderful'	SOF 252
'Lord, I lift your name on high'	SOF 897
'From heaven you came'	SOF 120
'So much'	BSBS2

Prayer idea

Remind everyone that Jesus chose to die on the cross so that our sins can be forgiven. Give out Post-it notes and, after prayers of confession, suggest people write or draw their thanks for Jesus' death and fix these on to a large cross. Pictures, symbols or initials can be used instead of words. Make a cardboard cross if you do not have a suitable wooden one. Thank God that we have been forgiven from all our sins through Jesus' death on the cross.

For a more sophisticated alternative, provide a large box, which, when opened out, makes the shape of a cross. The template can be downloaded from **web ref AASA3.starters_2**. In advance, fix the box into shape so that it is firm but can be undone easily. Everyone sticks their notes on the outside of the box. When this has been done, open out the box, displaying the cross.

Extra idea

Thinking of Jesus' self-sacrifice, spend time remembering people who live a life of possible danger, such as the police, medics and paramedics, lifeboat crews and soldiers. Download information about one such group of people. You could pray for them, or make posters for an exhibition, or hold a fund-raising event. If members of your congregation are in any of these professions, honour them particularly. Children might enjoy making a bravery medal for them.

Jesus' on trial

Bible passage: Matthew 26:57–68
Session aim: To identify the unfairness of Jesus' trial

Theme introduction

In advance, ask for help in acting out one or more of the following situations:

- Two children come in wearing torn or dirty clothes (eg muddy-looking Wellington boots). You ask where they have been and are told they have played in a forbidden place. One of them is told off very severely. The other is told, 'Never mind. I know you couldn't help it.'
- You are going to share out a bag of sweets among a group of children. However, you intentionally miss out some, but give others several sweets each.
- Two people are having an argument over the ownership of something. You intervene, saying you will find out who the real owner is. But you only listen to one person's side of the story and decide in their favour.

Ask everyone what was wrong with the acted-out situations: it was unfair! Explain that unfair things often happen, and it always upsets us. Even when the unfair thing happens in our favour, we don't feel good about it. Today the children will hear about something very unfair that happened to Jesus.

Prayer idea

Pray today for people in unfair situations around the world. Information and pictures could be obtained from organisations such as Christian Solidarity Worldwide or Tearfund. Show a PowerPoint, or put up posters or topic headings around the church, and allow people time to think and pray individually or in small groups. Have information available for people to take home in case they want to follow up with more support.

For more details of Christians under pressure, visit www.csw.org.uk. The International Day of Prayer for the Persecuted Church takes place on 8 November 2009 – for more details visit www.idop.org. You can get further information from Release International at www.releaseinternational.org or by typing 'imprisoned for Christian faith' into a search engine.

Extra idea

Supply cross-shaped bookmarks, one for each person (see **web ref AASA3.starters_3** for a template). Suggest everyone writes on one side, 'Thank you, Jesus' and on the other, puts names or draws a picture of people who are being treated unfairly, or places where there is unfair treatment – eg where food for starving people is not being distributed evenly, where a corrupt government is being biased towards some people, or where Christians are being persecuted for their faith. Suggest everybody takes their bookmark home to continue thanking Jesus for suffering for us and praying for people who are being treated unfairly.

Jesus saves

Bible passage: Matthew 27:15 – 28:20
Session aim: To rejoice that Jesus is the victor

Theme introduction

Hold up a cardboard cross with the long piece bent to make all the arms equal, as an X. Ask what this sign means, eg 'a special place' (on a map), 'wrong' (maths), 'love' (kiss), a crossroads (making a decision, or registering a vote in the ballot box).

Unfold the bent arm. Say that Jesus' cross is all the same things as above: it is a very special place; it reminds us that we have all done wrong; it tells us how much God loves us; and it is something we all have to make a decision about.

Today, however, we are celebrating because the cross is empty. Jesus died on it, but he came back to life.

Song suggestions

'Come on and celebrate'	SOF 73
'Jesus, we celebrate your victory'	SOF 309
'I believe in Jesus'	SOF 203
'In the tomb so cold they laid him'	SOF 245
'The word of the Lord is planted in my heart'	ks 338
'So much'	BSBS2

Prayer idea

Put a pile of large pebbles at the foot of a cross. These are to remind us of the stone put in front of the tomb where Jesus' body was laid. Ask everyone to come forward and take a pebble to remind them that the stone was rolled away when Jesus rose from death.

Allow time for everyone to write or draw praises on their stone. Together, thank God for his power and victory; then suggest the stones are put somewhere away from the cross, to remind everyone that Jesus is alive today.

Ask everyone to remember to take home their 'praise stone' at the end of the service.

Extra idea

An activity for Bible Sunday 25th October 2009: Before the service, prepare seven cards as below, and place in seven Bibles. Ask seven people to stand in a row, each holding a Bible with a card inside. They should take out the card and read loudly what it says. Each person should say the name of a different day of the week before reading the words about Bible literature. The words on the cards should read: 'The Bible contains… law', '… history', '… songs', '… letters', '… stories about Jesus', '… picture stories', '… prophecies.'

If necessary, explain what these different sorts of literature are. Such variety! Comment: 'Something for every day of the week!' Ask one of the group how many days there are in a year and another to look up how many pages there are in the Bible (check whether the numbering starts again at the beginning of the New Testament) and say, 'More than enough for every day of the year!' If appropriate, ask someone to talk about why they read the Bible regularly.

Display samples of Bible-reading material for all age groups and details of other Bible Sunday resources – visit www.scriptureunion.org.uk.

You could listen to this story from *The Big Bible Storybook* audio book, 'Easter Sunday'.

To help you explain the cross to an all-age congregation, get hold of *Top Tips on Explaining the Cross to Children and Young People* (SU). For more details see page 87.

Birth of a nation

God rescues his people from slavery in Egypt.

Learn and remember verse:
'This is the day of the Lord's victory; let us be happy, let us celebrate!'
Psalm 118:24

The song 'Let us celebrate' from *Bitesize Bible Songs 2*, puts these words to music and can be downloaded from www.scriptureunion.org.uk/light.

The all-age service outline that is part of this series is 'Trusting God in the tough times' on page 66, focusing on Exodus 5:1 – 6:13; 2 Corinthians 11:21b–31;12:8–10.

Oct – Dec
5

Rescue and run

Bible passage: Exodus 2: 1–25
Session aim: To discover that God uses unlikely people in his rescue plan

Theme introduction

If you know of someone in the congregation with a hidden talent (eg somebody who plays an unusual musical instrument, can do conjuring tricks, or who paints beautiful pictures), ask in advance if they would be willing to show or demonstrate their skill. After the demonstration, comment that if before this service, we had been thinking about music, conjuring or painting, we might never have imagined this unlikely person had such a talent. Say that God knows what he has gifted us with, and often uses unlikely people to do amazing things for him, as the children will discover in the story of Moses.

An alternative way to introduce the theme is to invite people of all ages from the congregation to announce a hymn, read the notices etc. Do not warn people in advance, but be careful about whom you choose. Follow this by saying that these people probably think they are the most unlikely ones to be introducing the service today. Similarly, God chooses unlikely people to help in his work.

Prayer idea

Ask everyone to think about the person sitting to their right. Can they imagine this person driving a train, sweeping the carpets at Buckingham Palace, singing solo at the local shops or giving the sermon? Some of these things will seem very unlikely. But God sometimes chooses some of the most unlikely people to do things for him. Suggest that everyone prays for the person on their right that they will be ready to say 'yes' to God, whatever he asks them to do for him.

In a similar way ask people to pray for the person on their left.

Extra idea

Ask two or three people to come to church in their work clothes. It would be good to choose those who wear a uniform for work, or dress in a business suit on weekdays but casually for church. Ask them to talk very briefly about their job and then give an example of how God has used them to do something for him in their work capacity.

You could listen to this story from *The Big Bible Storybook* audio book, 'Baby in a basket'.

Song suggestions

'Jesus put this song into our hearts'   SOF 299
'Brother, let me be your servant'   SOF 54
'I want to serve the purpose of God' SOF 260
'Let us celebrate'   BSBS2

Holy ground

Bible passage: Exodus 3:1 – 4:20
Session aim: To discover that God enables people to take part in his rescue plan

Theme introduction

Tell the Russian folk tale, 'The Tale of the Turnip'. An old man plants turnip seeds and one grows so big that he cannot pull it up. He asks his wife to put her arms round his waist and pull with him. They both pull, but to no avail; so they enlist, one at a time, a boy, a girl, a dog and a cat, all pulling in a long line. Still the turnip will not budge, until they ask a little mouse. With his added help the turnip is pulled up and everyone enjoys turnip soup. (*The Enormous Turnip* is published by Ladybird, among others, but a version can be easily downloaded using a search engine.)

The story could be acted out using people from the congregation (possibly with some animal masks), or as a series of simple pictures on PowerPoint. The point to get over, of course, is that every person who took part was important to the task. Similarly, God enables all sorts of people to help in his plan of salvation. Moses and his brother, Aaron, were to discover this.

Song suggestions

'Be still, for the presence of the Lord'	*SOF* 40
'Jesus bids us shine'	*ks2* 588
'Be Thou my vision'	*SOF* 42
'Everyone in the whole wide world'	*JP* 333
'Let us celebrate'	*BSBS2*

Prayer idea

One way we can all take part in God's work is to pray. All prayers are acceptable to God, just as all pray-ers are welcome. Announce topics for prayer, specific to the needs of the church, leaving them written up somewhere as a reminder.

Give out A5 paper, pens and scissors and ask everyone to draw round their hand and cut out its shape. (Keeping fingers together rather than outspread will make the whole exercise easier.) People should then write or draw their prayers on the cut-out hands, after which these should be glued or stapled together in a long chain. This streamer could be hung up or laid across the front of the church as a reminder of our part in God's work.

Extra idea

Cut the following large body shapes out of paper or card: a hand, a foot, a head, an arm and a leg (with the hand and foot attached). Write the name of your church on each shape.

Give out small Post-it notes. Ask everyone to write or draw the things they do or feel they are good at on separate notes, and then place these on the relevant part of the body. For instance, 'singing' would go near the mouth, 'counselling' on the ear, 'lifting heavy things' on the arm and 'visiting' on the feet. Help everyone to see that we all have a part to play in God's work in the church.

If you are participating in a service of Remembrance, you could use a military example of how different personnel perform a variety of jobs, from driving tanks and flying planes to caring for the wounded. There is a sense in which those involved in situations of war could be seen as rescuing civilians who have been treated unjustly, but you may not wish to make that connection. Make time to pray for all those involved in military conflict and those suffering in war-torn areas of the world in need of rescue.

You could listen to this story from *The Big Bible Storybook* audio book, 'God talks to Moses'.

Sacrificial lamb

Bible passage: Exodus 11:1 – 12:30

Session aim: To discover that God's people have to obey him as he rescues them

Theme introduction

In this series, as you engage with the story of the exodus, it would be good to remember that God is a God who rescues. Leviticus 26:1–6, 9–13 resonates with God's goodness and power as he rescued his people from Egypt and yet, God's words begin by reminding the people to obey God's laws. This reading can be split into two voices: 'Voice 1' speaks what God has done; 'Voice 2' tells what the people must do or will experience. As an introduction, remind everyone of the background to the story. Leviticus 26:1–6, 9–13 can be downloaded from **web ref AASA3.starters_4**.

As you read Leviticus 26:1–6, 9–13, two people should walk slowly from the back of church to the front. One (a slave) should be bowed down with a heavy burden, even chains, across their shoulders. At the end of the reading, when they are at the front, the other one should say, 'Give me your burden. Walk tall with your head held high.' The 'slave' does what they are told. Follow this with a song of praise to God with everyone standing up straight.

Song suggestions

'I want to walk with Jesus Christ'	SOF 261
'Just as I am'	SOF 316
'When we walk with the Lord'	SOF 599
'And can it be'	SOF 21
'Let us celebrate'	BSBS2

Prayer idea

Ask each person in a small group to link their arms as though making a chain.

Ask everyone to think of one time when they felt trapped or in need of being rescued, either literally or metaphorically. Pray, thanking God that he is with us at all times and in all difficulties, and is a God who rescues.

Then ask everyone to think of something that God may want them to do that is hard. Maybe they do not want to obey him. Offer some examples. Ask for God to help you all to do what is right. Then conclude by calling out: 'Lord God, set us free so that we can walk with our heads held high.'

At this point (and you will need to warn people not to hit anyone) everyone should fling their arms out wide and cry: 'We will trust and obey the Lord God.'

Extra idea

Re-enact the Passover story in family groups, with everyone wearing outdoor clothes as if ready to leave. Tell the story from Exodus 12 as the groups act it out (with pieces of roast lamb if you can manage it, and flat bread such as pitta). Make a brush from a bushy plant (eg heather) and fix paper around a doorway. Daub the paper with red paint, using the makeshift brush.

You could listen to this story from *The Big Bible Storybook* audio book, 'A meal to remember'.

The great escape

Bible passage: Exodus 14:1–31
Session aim: To recognise that God protects his people

Theme introduction

Create a selection of protective clothing such as hard hats/helmets, waterproof coats, cooks' aprons and oven gloves etc. Invite some of the children to put them on and say what the clothing is used for. Agree that they are for protecting people, but decide that they may not always work as well as we would like. Be sensitive concerning any situations known to people who might be present.

Explain that ultimately the only person who can protect us is God. The most amazing way he protected us, of course, is when Jesus died to save us from sin and separation from him. But he has protected his people at other times too, and today the children will be hearing a famous story about how this happened.

Song suggestions

'My Jesus, my Saviour'	SOF 935
'Faithful One, so unchanging'	SOF 89
'In heavenly armour'	SOF 237
'Safe in the shadow of the Lord'	SOF 991
'Let us celebrate'	BSBS2

Prayer idea

You will need a large shield of card, or a shield shape on a flip chart, an acetate or pre-prepared PowerPoint. Explain that a shield is an ancient means of protecting a soldier. Talk about this together.

Divide the shield up into four quarters, if possible, using children to help you. Identify four areas of life where people need to experience God's protection: for example, anyone who is travelling this week; anyone who has a dangerous job; anyone who is afraid; an international place of danger. These should be written on the shield and possibly illustrated with a symbol or photo: for example, a vehicle, a piece of protective clothing, a scared face and a marked map of the world. Then lead in prayer for these situations and people.

Extra idea

Give out A4 sheets of paper to everyone. Ask people to fold the sides into the middle landscape, thus creating two 'doors' that cover the centre. Then everyone should draw themselves or writes their name in the centre. Fold the doors across the picture. On the doors, they should write some of God's promises of protection from the Bible or phrases from some of today's suggested songs. To help, display Bible references such as Psalms 91 and 121 and the song numbers.

To encourage each other, the papers could be swapped around so that people write words for someone else. Encourage everyone to take the papers home to remind themselves that they are covered by God's protection.

You could listen to this story from *The Big Bible Storybook* audio book, 'Crossing the red sea'.

Christmas praise

Explore and enjoy the well-loved Christmas story through the praises of those who saw it happen.

Learn and remember verse:
'God showed his love for us by sending his only Son into the world, so that we might have life through him.' I John 4:9

The song 'God has a plan', from *Bitesize Bible Songs*, puts these words to music and can be downloaded from www.scriptureunion.org.uk/light.

The all-age service outline that is part of this series is an Advent service, 'Mary waits and waits', on page 71, focusing on Isaiah 9:6,7; Luke 1:26–45. An all-age nativity service outline, 'It's the nativity', is available on page 75, focusing upon Luke 1:26–38; Luke 2:1–20; John 1:1–18 or Isaiah 9:2–7.

Oct – Dec 9 — Zechariah's praise

Bible passage: Luke 1:67–80
Session aim: To explore how God gets his people ready for Jesus

Theme introduction

Ask a group of children to list all the things they would need to do to prepare for a party. They can do this during an introductory hymn or announcements. Then encourage the children to read out their list. Ask the congregation if they can think of anything that has been missed out. Would the children be ready for the party?

Hopefully, someone will notice that something has been forgotten. Comment that often we do forget important things in our planning, but God never forgets. When it came to preparing people for the coming of Jesus, he made very careful planning indeed.

Song suggestions

'O come, o come, Immanuel'	SOF 410
'Open our eyes, Lord'	ks 278
'Open the eyes of my heart, Lord'	SOF 1490
'God has a plan'	BSBS

Prayer idea

Use Luke 1:68–79 as a basis for prayer. In advance, choose five people to read some of the verses. After each section, develop your own prayers as suitable for your situation under the following headings:
Verses 68,69: Praise God for his saving power, and that he sent Jesus to live among us.
Verses 70,71: Thank God for the Bible.

Verses 72–75: Pray for your country, asking God to bless all who live in it, and to give wisdom to those who rule.
Verses 76,77: Thank God for those who pointed us on the way towards God. Pray for the church with the task of preaching the gospel.
Verses 78–80: Ask for God's light to shine in the dark places of the world, mentioning any relevant and topical situations.

Extra idea

This is the first Sunday of Advent. If you celebrate this season with an Advent wreath, remember to light the first candle today.

Children and adults could make their own Advent wreaths. Staple tinsel around the edge of a foil-covered paper plate. Tuck short lengths of ivy and other greenery under the tinsel. Use Blu-tack to fix four real or pretend white candles around the edge and one red one in the centre. Light one candle each Sunday and the last one on Christmas Eve. ('Light' pretend candles with a paper flame.)

Remind everybody that adults should supervise the lighting of candles and they should never be left unattended, especially when materials such as leaves are involved. After the service, give children whose parents were not present a written copy of this warning (see **web ref AASA3.starters_5**).

For more ideas for an Advent service, see the service outline on page 71.

Mary's praise

Bible passage: Luke 1:46–56
Session aim: To explore how Mary willingly accepted what God wanted

Theme introduction

There are some questions we would happily answer 'yes' to, and others to which we would emphatically answer 'no'. Ask for a show of hands (or perhaps ask people to stand up) to indicate who would answer 'yes' to the following questions:

Would you cook a meal for friends?
Would you paint a picture for someone?
Would you do someone's dirty washing?
Would you consider rowing across the Atlantic?
Would you dig up a worm and eat it?
Would you move to a smaller house for a better job?
Would you write a letter to tell someone they have done something good?

Explain that Mary was asked to agree to something unusual and difficult in today's story. Who asked her, and would she answer 'yes' or 'no'?

Song suggestions

'Make me a channel of your peace' *SOF* 381
'Father, I place into your hands'   *SOF* 97
'Over all the earth, you reign
  on high'   *SOF* 1498
'Let it be to me, according
  to your word'   *CP* 116
'God has a plan'   *BSBS*

Prayer idea

Teach the response, '**Help me to say "yes" to you.**' Then say the following prayer, with everyone responding after each section.

Lord God, when you ask me to do something that seems unusual or unnecessary…
Lord God, when you ask me to do something that is outside my comfort zone…
Lord God, when you ask me to do something that is going to be quite difficult for me to do…
Lord God, when you ask me to do something for someone I don't like very much…
Lord God, when you ask me to forgive when forgiveness is hard…

Extra idea

Form small groups of mixed ages. Make sure everyone has a copy of the same Bible version of Mary's song (Luke 1:46–55) and give each group one verse to learn by heart. (If you do not have enough groups, be ready to read the extra verses yourself.) Give everyone five minutes to practise saying their verse in whatever way they like: for example, all together, or a phrase each, or with actions or clapping. Check that each group is managing the task.

When everyone is ready, begin with 'Mary said…' and then let the groups say their verses in order. Say it through again, this time completely by heart with nobody looking at the 'crib sheet'!

Angels' praise

Bible passage: Luke 2:8–20
Session aim: To celebrate that God became human

Theme introduction

Ask three groups of young people, before the start of the service, to work out dramatic signs that demonstrate the meaning of the Learn and remember verse. 'God showed his love for us by sending his only Son into the world, so that we might have life through him.' 1 John 4:9.

Begin the service with all three groups showing their mini-drama. Speak appreciatively about all contributions and ensure that everyone says the verse at least twice. Comment that the children are going to celebrate that God himself became human.

Song suggestions

'Meekness and majesty'	SOF 390
'From heaven you came'	SOF 120
'Thou didst leave thy throne'	SOF 555
'Holy Child, how still you lie'	SOF 769
'God has a plan'	BSBS

Prayer idea

Cut out eight large letters in brightly coloured card, spelling IMMANUEL. If you have enough people to make more than eight small groups, include the letters for 'God with us'. Give each group a letter and glitter pens.

In their groups, ask everyone to think about how Jesus came to live on earth as one of us and to then write words of thanks and praise to him on the letter.

After a few minutes, ask representatives from each group to paste the letters in order on a long background strip of coloured or white paper.

Read out some of the phrases from each letter, with everyone responding each time, 'Thank you, Immanuel, for coming to be with us.'

Extra idea

Liaise with Social Services or a local charity and find out if there is a need for baby clothes in your area. If so, make a collection and pack parcels containing clothing and other appropriate baby items. Label whether the clothes are suitable for a boy or girl and the approximate age or size of the baby. Children could make gift cards to tie on the parcels. There are several national and international charities that work to provide parcels at Christmas to those in need. An Internet search engine will offer relevant information.

You could listen to this story from *The Big Bible Storybook* audio book, 'A message for shepherds'.

To think more about how you can explain to an all-age congregation how God became human, read *Top Tips on Explaining the Trinity to Young People* (SU).

Christmas praise

Bible passage: Luke 2:1–40
Session aim: To celebrate the birth of Jesus

Theme introduction

The following words can either be read aloud by two or more readers or displayed on a screen with the lines divided between sections of the congregation. Each line has four beats, which could be beaten on a drum or tambourine. This is also available as a download **web ref AASA3. starters_6**.

Begin by sharing any good news this week that is worth celebrating. Now listen to/join in with some very unusual good news which was a great cause for celebration.

Good news, good news, good news, good news!
Mary came to Bethlehem, so heavy and so tired,
But Joseph was beside her, her child was inside.
Good news, good news, the time has come!
Their accommodation they found, it was almost too late,
'Twas a good thing they did, for no baby would wait.
Good news, good news, the baby will come!
The baby was born, and in a manger, we are told
He was laid in the hay, to keep warm from the cold.
Good news, good news, the baby has come!
The skies, they were filled, with angels so bright,
And shepherds, in a rush, left their sheep in a fright!
Good news, good news, your Saviour is born!
They ran so very fast to catch sight of this child
Who, they had been told, had been born, Christ the Lord.
Good news, good news, our Saviour is born!
Good news, good news, our Saviour is born!

Song suggestions

'Come and join the celebration'	SOF 688
'I love the lights on the Christmas trees'	ks 137
'It was on a starry night'	SOF 1365
'Light for everyone'	LFE
'God has a plan'	BSBS

Prayer idea

Give each small group a party popper and a balloon (helium-filled ones would be especially good, but make sure they are firmly tied to a heavy object) and invite everyone to write celebratory praises and thanks for the birth of Jesus on the balloon.

Begin the prayer time by saying, 'We thank you, God, for the birth of Jesus, and we bring you our praises now.' The groups should then take turns to shout out the phrases on their balloon, while one member pulls the party popper. Everyone should respond each time with, 'We thank you, God, for Jesus!' Then, let out the string a little to allow the helium-filled balloons to float higher.

Extra idea

Decorate your worship area with strings of stars. To save time, buy ready-made star shapes (available from stationers' stores and often in fluorescent colours). If you want to make your own, a template is available at **web ref AASA3. starters_7**. Ask everyone to decorate several stars quite quickly rather than one very special one. Provide sparkly pens and small peel-off stars. Glitter glue will dry fairly quickly if spread thinly (use cocktail sticks to spread out a blob). Tape finished stars along brightly coloured yarn and hang them between pillars or along walls. Tails of stars would look good hanging from the balloons used in the prayer activity.

There is an all-age nativity service outline, 'It's the nativity', on page 75.

You could listen to this story from *The Big Bible Storybook* audio book, 'Jesus is born'.

Simeon's praise

Bible passage: Luke 2:28–35
Session aim: To thank God that he sent Jesus for all people

Theme introduction

Bring to the service any Christmas cards that you have received from other parts of the world and ask other people to do the same. Point out your own country on a globe or map of the world. Show a card from a country not too far away. Ask one of the children to mark this place on the map with a Post-it note, flag or sticker. Then challenge someone to show a card from somewhere a bit further away. Gradually discover who has greetings from the furthest distance, while marking all the places on the map.

Comment that all the people who sent cards from around the world are people whom Jesus came to earth for. Today we are going to thank him for that, and rejoice that we are also people he came for.

Song suggestions

'One shall tell another'	SOF 439
'I, the Lord of sea and sky'	SOF 830
'Let all the world'	SOF 879
'God has a plan'	BSBS

Prayer idea

Make a huge card showing a picture of Jesus in the manger (a picture to enlarge is available at **web ref AASA3.starters_8**) and the words 'Thank you for coming for all the people on earth.' Pass the card around the congregation, perhaps during a suitable hymn, and ask everyone to sign it. (Or you could use Post-it notes to stick inside.) If anyone knows the word for 'thank you' in another language, they should include that too. Bring the card to the front of the church. As it is held up, all say together, 'Thank you, Jesus, for coming to earth for all people.'

Extra idea

Elderly people have much to give (see the story of Simeon and Anna in Luke 2) but are often sidelined and forgotten. Challenge the members of your church to think of ways the elderly could be helped to feel special and useful. For instance,

they could be part of a prayer chain that prays specifically for those who preach on Sunday, or the leaders of children's groups. The preachers could get in touch with the pray-ers, letting them know the verses they will be speaking on, and the aim of the sermon. A 'shut-in' would feel they had a definite part to play in the service even if they could not attend.

You could listen to this story from *The Big Bible Storybook* audio book, 'Simeon and Anna'.

If the children have already heard the story of Simeon and read Luke 2:28–35, you could show the wordsearch below, also available from **web ref AASA3.starters_9**, asking everyone to find the words in the Bible passage and then in the wordsearch. (The electronic version can be completed by clicking on screen.) Use the leftover letters to complete this sentence:

It was _ _ _'_   _ _ _ _ that Jesus should come for all people.

G	S	O	G	R	D	N
F	A	L	L	I	N	G
S	V	I	O	S	I	I
E	I	G	R	I	A	S
P	O	H	Y	N	P	P
O	U	T	L	G	A	N
H	R	E	V	E	A	L

SAVIOUR	GLORY	LIGHT
FALLING	REVEAL	SIGN
RISING	PAIN	HOPE

Travelling in faith

The first followers of Jesus find their lives turned upside down but they know that Jesus is always with them.

Learn and remember verse:
'Now God's home is with human beings! He will live with them, and they shall be his people.' Revelation 21:3a

The song 'Now God's home', from *Bitesize Bible Songs 2,* puts these words to music and can be downloaded from www.scriptureunion.org.uk/light.

The all-age service outline that is part of this series is 'New Year resolution: Share Jesus!' on page 79, focusing on Genesis 12:1–5; Acts 16:6–10.

Starting out

Bible passage: Acts 13:1–52
Session aim: To see how God sends and goes with his people

Jan – Mar
1

Theme introduction

Wish everyone a happy new year! Then 'wonder' why, early in January, we do this. Listen to a few answers from adults and children and conclude that it is a good thing to hope that everyone will be happy in the coming year.

Get out your new diary and pretend to look through it. Note that there are things in it that you are not looking forward to. Perhaps other people feel the same… Some may have exams or operations to face, or other events that might be difficult. And we don't know what unseen problems and difficulties lie ahead. No one can guarantee to be happy all year!

So why do we all cheerfully wish each other 'Happy New Year!'? Comment that, although we don't know the future, we are certain of one important thing. Whatever happens, Jesus will be with us. Who knows, he may turn our lives upside down in the coming year! Jesus will most certainly be right beside us all the way. The children are going to hear how God went with the apostle Paul at the start of his travels.

Song suggestions

'Now God's home'	BSBS2
'Be bold, be strong'	ts 38
'Father, I place into your hands'	ts 97
'I walk by faith'	ts 253
'I'm gonna trust in God'	SOF 1339

Prayer idea

Give out foot-shaped pieces of paper. Invite everyone to write or draw on the shape something that they are either looking forward to or fearing in the year ahead. When this is done, ask everyone to hold up their shapes to say together, 'Jesus goes with me!'

Extra idea

This week's Bible passage recounts how Paul and Barnabas were set apart for their mission work; so it would be very appropriate to hold an informal commissioning for the coming year. Invite those in various categories to stand or raise their hands in turn. Make the categories as inclusive as possible – for example, those who are at school or studying, those who are starting new ventures, those who pray regularly for others, those who do voluntary work, those who support campaigns which help people in need and, finally, everyone who is seeking to serve Christ and live God's way.

After people in each category have raised their hands, pray briefly or say, 'We set you apart for the work God has called you to do.'

You could listen to this story from *The Big Bible Storybook* audio book, 'Paul helps Barnabas'.

Hard times

Bible passage: Acts 14:1–28

Session aim: To discover how God helps his people bravely speak for him

Theme introduction

Hold a 'speak out'. Ask three or four prepared people (adults and children) to speak for only 30 seconds on an issue about which they are passionate – perhaps something like fair trade, caring for the elderly, a healthy lifestyle or even something like trainspotting! Make sure that the speakers keep to time, and encourage the congregation to applaud enthusiastically after each speech.

Gauge the general reaction to the speakers. How do people feel after hearing them speak so passionately on issues they greatly care about? There may be a range of reactions, but try to draw out that we feel 'stirred up' when we hear this kind of thing; we admire the courage of those who speak out, whether we agree or disagree.

Point out that when Paul and Barnabas spoke out about Jesus, they knew that people would be 'stirred up'. They did not know whether anyone would respond positively and they must have known that those who didn't want to hear the message might get angry and even violent. The children will hear more about this in their groups.

Song suggestions

'From the sun's rising'	ts 116
'I believe in Jesus'	ts 195
'I, the Lord of sea and sky'	ts 246
'We'll walk the land'	ts 551
'Tell the world'	SOF 1527
'Now God's home'	BSBS2

Prayer idea

Pray for those who are spreading the good news of Jesus or speaking out for truth and justice in the world. Either make a PowerPoint presentation with images from mission or news websites, or distribute cuttings from newspapers, mission journals and magazines. You should make a special mention of any mission partners who are supported by the church. Ask everyone to look at the images and pray in small groups that God will help people to bravely speak for him.

Extra idea

Alongside a reading of Acts 14:15–17 (the good news message that Paul and Barnabas gave in Lystra), work out a set of illustrative movements that could be performed by a group of people or taught to the whole congregation.

How welcoming are your all-age services to those who have not grown up in the church, especially children and young people? How far do the services work for those who do not naturally engage with written words? These two *Top Tips* titles will inspire and challenge you.

Reaching Unchurched Children
978 1 84427 127 6

Communicating God in Non-Book Ways
978 1 84427 329 4

For more details go to
www.scriptureunion.org.uk/shop

The church grows

Bible passage: Acts 16:1–15
Session aim: To know that God is with his people as we meet together

Theme introduction

Using sensitivity and your knowledge of the congregation, say that you notice a few people are missing. Perhaps someone is ill. You miss hearing them singing so well. Or maybe you miss a baby who has a lovely smile, or a child who likes helping give out books.

Ask everyone to think who would be missed most if they didn't come to church. Of course, it is God! We miss seeing our friends at church if they don't come, but so much would be different if we weren't sure that God would be present! Unless you have a small congregation (in which case do the exercise together), put everyone, children included, into groups to talk about what would be different if God was not in church. Feed back some of the conclusions.

Observe that there would be no meaning to our worship. Our worship is all about God's presence – knowing he is there. But because we know God is with us we can be sure that he welcomes us, blesses us, hears our prayers, speaks to us and so much more. Follow this with a time of silent prayer as each person thanks God that he is present during this service.

Song suggestions

'Almighty God'	SOF 1165
'Come down, O love divine'	SOF 1202
'As we are gathered'	ts 29
'He is here'	ts 157
'Be still and know'	JP 22
'Now God's home'	BSBS2

Prayer idea

Pray for members of the congregation who are not present today. Ask that the Holy Spirit will make God's presence known to them wherever they are. You could arrange for those who are ill, housebound or in need to be visited during the week, or at least organise that cards be sent assuring them of the church's love and prayers.

You could pray especially for any students who have recently gone back to university or college, asking them to send a personal message to everyone in church. Emails or letters could be sent to them in return.

Extra idea

If this is possible in your building, label the four walls or corners 'north', 'south', 'east' and 'west'. Ask everyone to go to the corner where they live in relation to the church. You may need to identify which roads or local districts are situated on or near the compass points. As you sing a song such as 'As we are gathered', everyone should slowly walk to a central point where a symbol of God is placed. This could be a cross, the Bible, a dove, a candle or just the word 'God'. You are gathering together to meet with God. (Alternatively, just a few representative people could do this.) Thank God that you can come together in this way, confident that he is there. Close by reading Psalm 139:7–12.

You could listen to this story from *The Big Bible Storybook* audio book, 'Lydia joins the church'.

Prison praise

Bible passage: Acts 16:16–40

Session aim: To be confident that God is with his people in challenging times

Theme introduction

Arrange a series of challenges – for example, saying the first lines of 12 Christmas carols in a minute; running up and down the room in a given time; keeping a balloon in the air for as long as possible; singing one song to the tune of another; putting dried peas into a jar with chopsticks. Make them as crazy as you like!

Ask for volunteers to take part in the challenges, choosing people of different ages and abilities. As the volunteers do their challenges in turn, encourage everyone to cheer them on. Thank them and ask how much it helped, having the encouragement of those watching. In their groups, the children will hear how Paul and Silas faced some really serious challenges but God was with them helping and encouraging them.

Song suggestions

'Do not be afraid'	SOF 1213
'Jesus, be the centre'	SOF 1377
'When the road is rough and steep'	SOF 1612
'Give thanks with a grateful heart'	ts 118
'Our confidence is in the Lord'	ts 417
'Now God's home'	BSBS2

Prayer idea

Pray for those who are in prison. For appropriate information, visit www.prisonfellowship.org.uk, especially the Angel Tree project. As this is an all-age part of the service, pray especially for children whose parents are in prison and for Christian prisoners who want to be involved in the upbringing of their children, developing good relationships with them, while being physically absent. May they experience God with them in this challenging time. Be very sensitive to the personal situations of anyone in the congregation, making sure you do not embarrass anyone.

Extra idea

As a way of affirming God's presence in each situation, think about the challenges that people of various ages face in their everyday life. Ask different groups to think of challenges that face small children, those at school, parents juggling home and work, those with the challenges of disability, the bereaved, the unemployed, those with pressurised jobs, the retired and the very elderly. Affirm that God is present with us in our day-to-day challenges as well as in more newsworthy ones.

You could listen to this story from *The Big Bible Storybook* audio book, 'Paul and Silas'.

Let's praise

Bible passage: Psalm 95:1–7
Session aim: To enjoy praising God

Theme introduction

Create an atmosphere for praise by asking the congregation to discuss, either in small groups or all together, what makes them say, 'Wow!' Give a couple of examples yourself to set them thinking – a sunset, a juggler, a butterfly, or whatever amazes you. Encourage people of all ages to tell others what has the 'Wow!' factor for them.

Long ago, people like us often looked at the world around them and were amazed. The book of Psalms is a collection of what they said, sang or wrote as they reflected on how great God is. Psalm 95 encourages us to say, 'Wow!' and then to say, 'We praise you, God!'

Conclude with a shout of praise. Divide the congregation into sectors. As you point at each sector in turn, everyone in that part of the room should shout out something that has the 'Wow!' factor for them. Everyone else should respond by shouting, 'We praise you, Lord!' Encourage energy and enthusiasm!

Song suggestions

'All heaven declares'	*ts* 8
'I reach up high'	*ts* 235
'I will enter his gates'	*ts* 262
'For the beauty of the earth'	*JP* 48
'I will wave my hands'	*JP* 376
'Wonderful, so wonderful'	*SOF* 1632

Prayer idea

Use the verses of Psalm 95:1–7, as shown below, in the way they were originally used in worship – as a congregational 'dialogue'. Display the words on PowerPoint or on the service sheet. To make the 'dialogue' as dynamic as possible, one half of the congregation should say the first part of each verse, and the other half reply with the second part. Small children could be given strips of crepe paper to wave as their contribution to the praise.

Come, let us sing for joy to the LORD;
let us shout aloud to the Rock of our salvation.
Let us come before him with thanksgiving

and extol him with music and song.
For the LORD is the great God,
the great King above all gods.
In his hand are the depths of the earth,
and the mountain peaks belong to him.
The sea is his, for he made it,
and his hands formed the dry land.
Come, let us bow down in worship,
let us kneel before the LORD our Maker;
for he is our God and we are the people of his pasture,
the flock under his care.

Extra idea

Make a PowerPoint presentation (or download the presentation from **web ref AASA3. starters_10**) to be shown alongside a reading of Psalm 95:1–7. Arrange for suitable upbeat music to be played during the reading. The reader should read slowly, allowing time for the pictures to be viewed and the words taken in.

Life in the desert

Follow Moses and the people of God as they journey in the desert, experiencing God's generous provision in all they do.

Learn and remember verse:
'He supplies the needs of those who honour him; he hears their cries and saves them.' Psalm 145:19

The song 'He supplies', from *Bitesize Bible Songs 2,* puts these words to music and can be downloaded from www.scriptureunion.org.uk/light.

The all-age service outline that is part of this series is 'God is so generous' on page 83, focusing on Exodus 15:1–27; John 4:3–14.

Jan – Mar 6

Bread and water

Bible passage: Exodus 16:1–36; 17:1–7

Session aim: To recognise how God provides for his people

Theme introduction

Write the letters GOD PROVIDES on separate large cards. In this quiz, the first letter of each answer spells out GOD PROVIDES:

What fruit is used to make wine?	**G**RAPES
What vegetable makes you cry?	**O**NION
Which sticky fruit grows on palm trees?	**D**ATE
Hilo, Kona Sugarloaf and Natal Queen are all varieties of which fruit?	**P**INEAPPLE
What is the staple food for people in Asia?	**R**ICE
Which colour in the rainbow comes between red and yellow?	**O**RANGE
What is added to baking soda to make a home-made volcano?	**V**INEGAR
What is frozen water called?	**I**CE
Orangeade, cider and tea are all kinds of what?	**D**RINK
What symbol of new life is given to children at Easter?	**E**GGS
According to the nursery rhyme, what are little girls made of?	**S**UGAR AND SPICE

After the quiz, ask if anyone knows what the answers had in common. (They are all things God provides!)

Song suggestions

'Beauty for brokenness'	ts 37
'O give thanks to the Lord'	ts 384
'The birds don't worry'	SOF 1532
'For the fruits of his creation'	SOF 1234
'Yes, God is good'	JP 293
'He supplies'	BSBS 2

Prayer idea

Everyone joins in the emboldened response:
Lord God, you are generous.
Please help us to be generous too.
Our shops are full of things to eat and drink because you are generous to us.
Please help us to be generous too.
In our towns and cities, there are many places to eat because you are generous to us.
Please help us to be generous too.
At home, we can enjoy our meals and never really go hungry because you are generous to us.
Please help us to be generous too.
Help us to remember those in need and share the good things you have given us.
Please help us to be generous too.

Extra idea

If you already have a fair trade stall, make this available and encourage people to support it. Otherwise, invite a local fair trade supplier to show what is available. This is a way of celebrating God's generosity to us and helping others have a fair share of what he provides.

If this Sunday is Education Sunday, you may wish to pray for all those involved in education – students, staff, parents or governors. For more details visit www.educationsunday.org.

You could listen to this story from the *Big Bible Storybook* audio book, 'Living in the desert'.

Laws for life

Bible passage: Exodus 19:16 – 20:17
Session aim: To see how God's rules show the best way of living

Theme introduction

Invite a couple of volunteers to play a simple game with rules. The 'Yes/No' game would be suitable. Make the rules plain: the players must take turns to answer your questions using words (no shaking or nodding heads) and they must not say 'yes' or 'no'. If they break either rule, they are out.

After the game, discuss the rules. They were very simple, but hard to keep! But comment that without them, there would be no game.

Talk about God's rules for living. They are simple – loving God with all your heart, not stealing, killing or lying and so on – but seem to be very hard to keep. Why does God give us rules that are so hard? Why doesn't he give us easy rules like 'Eat chocolate every day' or 'Do what you like as long as it makes you happy' or 'Take what you like from other people'?

Conclude that God's rules are for our benefit. They are in fact a result of how much he loves us. (You could comment on different sorts of love, in the light of Valentine's Day.) God's rules show us the very best way of living, so that we are all happy. Without God's rules, life would be very sad for everyone. The children are going to discover more about God's laws for life.

Song suggestions

'Faithful God'	*ts* 88
'I give you all the honour'	*ts* 203
'Restore, O Lord'	*ts* 439
'You call us first'	SOF 1658
'Seek ye first'	JP 215
'He supplies'	BSBS 2

Prayer idea

Find headlines in local newspapers that illustrate the damage that occurs when God's rules are broken (nothing too graphic!). Headlines can be scanned into a computer and displayed on PowerPoint, or cut out and distributed to small groups in the congregation.

Allow time for these headlines to be discussed, encouraging adults to ask children what they think about what is happening locally that spoils life for other people. Allow time for groups to pray together about these issues.

Extra idea

Give out Valentine's cards with a red heart and the words 'I love you' on the front. Inside, paste a printed piece of paper headed 'God's loving rules' and underneath Jesus' summary of the Law (Matthew 22:37–40). Explain that God wants us to keep his rules because he knows they will make us happy. They are his way of saying, 'I love you'.

You could listen to this story from *The Big Bible Storybook* audio book, 'Rules from God'.

Moses meets God

Bible passage: Exodus 33:7–23; 34:1–9, 29–35
Session aim: To wonder at the awesomeness of God

Theme introduction

Briefly describe an awe-inspiring building that you have visited (a church or cathedral would be ideal), showing pictures if possible. Explain how the grandeur or beauty of the building affected you.

The people of Israel had a place like that when they were in the desert – they called it the Tent of the Lord's Presence. It was a place of meeting with God – just as the building where you are at present is a place of meeting with God. The Tent of the Lord's Presence was beautiful, even though it was just a tent – somewhere that reminded the people just how awesome God is. Read Exodus 34:5–7, in which God comes down to his people in a cloud and describes himself. Use the PA system so that the reader is not seen and play some very grand background music or a roll of the drums which gets louder by the end of verse 5.

With the music still playing (and you will need to get the timing right), give people some space to think about and imagine how awesome God is. The children will discover more about his awesomeness in their group session.

Song suggestions

'Ascribe greatness'	ts 25
'God of glory'	ts 130
'Our God is an awesome God'	ts 418
'Immortal, invisible'	ts 220
'Holy, holy, holy'	SOF 1281
'He supplies'	BSBS 2

Prayer idea

Set up six stations around the building, each with a bowl or basket. Place labels beside five of these baskets which say: 'God is merciful'; 'God is very patient'; 'God shows great love'; 'God can be trusted'; 'God keeps his promises for ever'. (These words are based on Exodus 34:6,7 CEV.) At the sixth, which should be central, put tokens – such as flower petals, stones or leaves – in the bowl. Encourage people to walk around thinking about who God is. They can place a token in the bowl beside any label that strikes them as especially important for their lives at present.

Extra idea

Take extra care to prepare the room for worship. This could be done with the help of children or a group of people of any age who would enjoy making the room beautiful. They might use drapes, flowers, pictures, banners, perfume or anything else they choose to inspire a sense of awe.

You could listen to this story from *The Big Bible Storybook* audio book, 'Moses meets God'.

Giving to God

Bible passage: Exodus 35:20 – 36:7; 39:32 – 40:38

Session aim: To enjoy giving to God in worship

Theme introduction

Ask everyone to imagine God's people living in the desert. They had no buildings for their worship. They were just beginning to find out how awesome God is and they wanted a place that would remind them of this. They did not have lots of possessions – they had to carry everything they owned. What could they do to make their place of worship fit for such a great God?

They brought the best they had – decorative pins, earrings, rings, necklaces, gold jewellery, fine linen; blue, purple or red wool; cloth of goats' hair; rams' skin dyed red; fine leather; gold thread; acacia wood; jewels, spices and perfumed oil! But they didn't just bring their possessions. They also brought the talents God had given them: artistic skill, ability and understanding, engraving, designing, weaving, embroidery, building, leather work, woodwork, metalwork!

Show items to represent some of the items and skills. Invite people to hold these up. Enjoy the richness of what we can offer God in worship. Ask what the congregation has brought to this service to worship this great God. Encourage everyone to think of something and tell those around them. It could be a voice to sing, a willingness to help, enthusiasm, energy or any kind of skill or service.

Prayer idea

Pray that God will help you enrich the worship you offer to him. Mention a few of the gifts that might be offered, focusing on things that anyone can bring – gifts of joy; enthusiasm; willingness to serve and help and welcome; decorating and caring for the premises; as well as 'upfront' skills. Make sure that you include younger children in this. Invite everyone to dedicate their gifts to God by including a time of reflection, after which you say, 'Great and wonderful God, we offer you the gifts and skills we have thought about. Help us to use them as we come to worship you.' You could incorporate the taking of the monetary offering during this time.

Extra idea

Give out strips of blue, purple and red fabric/ crepe paper. Explain that these represent the possessions, skills and abilities we have brought to worship our great God. These can be brought forward joyfully as an offering and draped to decorate any suitable place at the front of the room. You could set up a branch with bare twigs for the purpose.

Song suggestions

'Be glorified'	ts 42
'Come on and celebrate'	ts 75
'Praise my soul, the King of heaven'	ts 433
'This is my desire'	SOF 1561
'O! O! O! how good is the Lord'	JP 180
'He supplies'	BSBS 2

Light for life

Be inspired, challenged and encouraged as you explore the Bible's images of light.

Learn and remember verse:
'The people who lived in darkness have seen a great light.
They lived in a land of shadows, but now light is shining on them.' Isaiah 9:2

The song 'Shining', from *Bitesize Bible Songs 2*, puts these words to music and can be downloaded from www.scriptureunion.org.uk/light.

The all-age service outline that is part of this series is 'Shining like stars' on page 89, focusing on Philippians 2:14–16; 1 Kings 19:9–15.

Jan – Mar 10

Light to live by

Bible passage: Psalm 119:9–16,105
Session aim: To discover that God's Word shows us how to live

Theme introduction

How many ways have people used light today? Without light, the world would be in darkness. How amazing that our planet has a moon so that the sun's light is reflected to us even at night! The moon's light helps us see in the darkness.

Hold up a Bible and ask how the Bible is like the moon. (Make it clear that the Bible is like a light in the darkness, helping us see God's ways. Without the Bible, it would be like stumbling along in the dark, with no clear idea of what God was saying.)

Learn Psalm 119:105 together, using these actions: 'Your word (*palms form an open book*) is a lamp (*mime holding lamp*) to guide me (*point ahead*) and a light (*mime holding torch*) for my path (*point at feet*). Say this several times, perhaps with different groups saying it in turn.

Song suggestions

'Jesus, you're my firm foundation'	ts 302
'Seek ye first'	ts 447
'Father, your word'	JP 338
'Thou, whose almighty word'	SOF 554
'Thy word is a lamp unto my feet'	SOF 1066
'Shining'	BSBS2

Prayer idea

If possible, darken the room. In this prayer of confession, each time the congregation says the response, **Let the light of your Word shine in our hearts**, turn on a spotlight or powerful torch. Then switch it off during the words that follow.

Lord God, your Word is like a light in the darkness, but we have often preferred to live in the darkness. From now on…
Let the light of your Word shine in our hearts.
We admit we haven't always taken the trouble to listen to your Word. From now on…
Let the light of your Word shine in our hearts.
We are sorry for times when we haven't taken pleasure in your Word. From now on…
Let the light of your Word shine in our hearts.

Extra idea

The Bible cannot be a light to us if we don't read it. Challenge everyone to read (or listen to) part of the Bible every day this week, perhaps verses from Psalm 119. Each day, parents could read a Bible story to their small children..

For more ideas to help parents nurture the faith of their children, visit www.scriptureunion.org.uk/ families or read *Families with faith: Survival skills for Christian parents* by Richard Patterson (SU).

In 2010, 7th March is Tearfund Sunday, seeking to bring God's light and justice into a dark world. To find out more, visit www.tearfund.org.

Is seeing believing?

Bible passage: John (8:12) 9:1–12, 35–38;
Session aim: To recognise who Jesus is

Theme introduction

Gather some interesting facts about the sun – what it is, its size, how far away it is and so on (www.hao.ucar.edu/Public/education/basic. html is very child-friendly). Try to engender an atmosphere of amazement at the power of the sun.

The sun is the main source of light for the world. We couldn't live without it. In Jesus' day, they did not know the scientific facts about the sun, but Jesus knew how vital it was for all life on earth. Perhaps this is what he had in mind when he said: 'I am the light of the world. Whoever follows me will have the light of life and will never walk in darkness' John 8:12.

Help everyone learn this verse. Divide the congregation into seven sections and do a Mexican wave. Begin by saying together, 'Jesus said…' Then let each section in turn raise their arms saying one word to complete the sentence, 'I am the light of the world'. Then all say together the rest of the verse. Repeat several times. Alternatively, use the song 'Follow me' from *Bitesize Bible Songs* which is a *Learn and remember* verse version of John 8:12.

Song suggestions

'Great is the darkness'	ts 136
'Jesus, how lovely you are'	ts 276
'Shine bright'	JP 453
'Christ, whose glory fills the sky'	SOF 1200
'Light of the world'	SOF 1419
'Shining'	BSBS2
'Follow me'	BBS

Prayer idea

John 8:12 records Jesus' promise that his followers will never walk in darkness. Collect ideas from the congregation about situations in which they feel as though they are in darkness. Then weave these into a prayer asking Jesus to shine the light of his presence into situations that seem difficult at the moment.

Extra idea

Create an instant banner. Before the service, draw a large circle in pencil to fill a large piece of black or blue card. In orange or yellow lettering, put the words 'Jesus, light of the world' inside the circle. Cut yellow and orange strips of paper into rectangles to be rays of the sun and give everyone a few. As they leave the building, they could use glue sticks to paste their pieces of paper around the circle to create a sun.

A smaller version could be created by children to give as a gift to their mother as a reminder of this service if this is Mothering Sunday. There are ideas for Mothering Sunday in the all-age service on page 93.

You are light

Bible passage: Matthew 5:14–16
Session aim: To be encouraged to be light for others

Theme introduction

Comment on whether or not it has been good weather recently for stargazing. Ask about the appeal of stars and gather thoughts about how it feels to look into the sky and see those pinpricks of light. You could ask younger children if they know a song about stars and sing that. If possible, show some images on the screen of stars and constellations.

The children are going to explore some Bible verses that tell followers of Jesus to 'shine … like stars lighting up the sky' (see Philippians 2:14–16). Read these verses; then explain that this means they are to be like Jesus, bringing light, hope and goodness into the dark places of the world. This could be at home, in school or at work, in the neighbourhood or in places far away.

Song suggestions

'Filled with compassion'	ts 105
'We are marching'	ts 539
'I love you, Lord'	SOF 1329
'Shine your light on us'	SOF 1513
'I'm going to shine, shine, shine'	JP 392
'Shining'	BSBS2

Prayer idea

It would be appropriate to pray for projects run by or supported by your church, including secular ones and inter-church ventures. Ideally, display photographs to bring the work to life for anyone who is not closely involved. Try to ensure that children realise they are people who can be light for others. The projects they work for and pray for should be included in the prayers.

Extra idea

Interview someone in the congregation who is seeking to make a difference for God in their everyday life, shining like a star. Prepare this in advance so that the language used is jargon-free and appropriate for children, and, everyone can connect with what is said.

Give each person an adhesive star to wear on their clothes to remind them to 'Go and let your light shine'.

You could listen to this story from *The Big Bible Storybook* audio book, 'Light for the whole world'.

Into Jerusalem

Bible passage: Mark 11:1–11
Session aim: To see how Jesus starts his Easter journey

Theme introduction

Show three symbols from Mark 11:1–11: a rope, a coat (or cloak) and a palm branch (any leafy branch will do). Either give the fuller explanation as below or simply say that these symbols are all going to play a part in the Palm Sunday story. For the fuller version, read Mark 11:1–11 and ask what part the rope has in the story. (Refer to vs 2–4.) The donkey colt was tied with rope and led away for Jesus to ride on. A few days later, Jesus was led away to die! The Easter journey he was beginning would lead to the cross. Unlike the donkey, which had no choice, Jesus chose the journey, knowing what it would mean.

Look at the coat and 'discover' its part in the story (v 8). The crowd threw down their clothes to show that they realised what was happening – their king was entering Jerusalem. Only a few days later, Jesus' clothes would be taken from him and he would die like a criminal. Jesus knew what his entry into Jerusalem would mean, but continued on his journey anyway.

Discuss the branch in the same way. This represents the crowd's excitement and praise (vs 8,9). They didn't know how Jesus' Easter journey would end, but they knew something really important was happening. It does not matter how many or how few times we have heard the Easter story, we can praise God that Jesus saw his journey to its end.

Prayer idea

Encourage everyone to pray for those known to them who have never heard the Easter story. Pray that God will lead them on a journey of discovery so that they will know more about Jesus the King who willingly suffered and died for them. In particular, pray for children in schools who may have heard the story in a new way this year.

Extra idea

The crowd laid down their coats because they recognised Jesus as their King. Invite the congregation to do the same, perhaps along the aisle or front of the room, during the singing of a Palm Sunday hymn. Encourage everyone to do this with reverence as a sign of commitment to Jesus.

You could listen to this story from *The Big Bible Storybook* audio book, 'Palm Sunday'.

Song suggestions

'Come, let us worship Jesus'	*ts* 73
'Welcome the King'	*ts* 549
'You are the King of glory'	*SOF* 630
'All glory, laud and honour'	*SOF* 1157
'Hosanna, hosanna'	*JP* 365
'Make way, make way'	*SOF* 384

Risen!

Bible passage: Mark 16:1–8

Session aim: To see how the Easter story continues

Theme introduction

Introduce the idea that some journeys can be very difficult, but ultimately worthwhile. Briefly tell a story of your own to illustrate this.

Explain how Jesus' Easter journey, which began with his entry into Jerusalem on a donkey, became very difficult indeed. For Jesus, of course, it was the hardest journey anyone has ever had to make – but it was also difficult for his followers and family. How was it going to end? Recount simply the events leading up to the death of Jesus. Conclude with a reading of Mark 16:1–8 with a narrator, the women and the man in white.

This is a surprising ending! Where is the joy and celebration? It seems that the difficult journey had not ended for Jesus' followers when they heard that he was alive again. They were upset and terrified! It seems to have taken a while for the wonderful news to sink in. The children will hear more of this story.

All-age service outlines for Good Friday and for Easter Day are available on the *Light* website as a *Light for the Lectionary* download.

Song suggestions

'Celebrate Jesus'	ts 67
'In the tomb so cold'	ts 234
'O, what a morning'	ts 424
'Thine be the glory'	ts 510
'Low in the grave he lay'	ts 345
'Sing and celebrate (Easter)'	JP 457

Prayer idea

Think of people and communities who need to know Jesus is alive. As you pray for each one, say, for example, 'In *our town*…' and let everyone respond: 'Jesus is risen indeed!'

Extra idea

As a way of allowing the realisation that Jesus is alive to sink in deeply, say, rather than sing, an Easter hymn. For example, have a prepared group of speakers say the verses of 'O, what a morning', *the source* 424. Everyone can respond joyfully, saying the chorus as a praise shout.

You could listen to this story from *The Big Bible Storybook* audio book, 'Easter Sunday'.

How is your all-age service developing links into the community? Currently, there are unprecedented opportunities to support your local schools. This Top Tips title provides valuable information but also practical suggestions for building bridges.

Developing Partnerships Between Church and School
978 1 84427 339 3

It's Your Move, is one of three SU books that many churches give to their local schools. *It's Your Move* helps students prepare to move to secondary school, *Get Ready Go!* is for those about to enter foundation stage and *Life, Actually* is for those aged 15 or 16 making the big decisions in life.

It's Your Move
978 1 84427 212 5 (Single copy)
978 1 84427 213 3 (Pack of 10)

Get Ready, Go!
978 1 84427 132 3 (Single copy)
978 1 84427 133 1 (Pack of 10)

Life, Actually
978 1 84427 116 1 (Single copy)
978 1 84427 148 X (Pack of 10)

Joshua

Joshua discovers that, with God's help, anything is possible because God is powerful.

Learn and remember verse:
'Don't be afraid or discouraged, for I, the Lord your God, am with you wherever you go.' Joshua 1:9b

The song, 'I am with you', from *Bitesize Bible Songs*, puts these words to music and can be downloaded from www.scriptureunion.org.uk/light. Additional ideas for learning this verse can be found on **web ref AASA3.starters_11**.

The all-age service outline that is part of this series is 'Remember, remember' on page 97, focusing on Joshua 4:1–24; Luke 22:7–20; 1 Corinthians 11:23–26.

Always there

April – June

2

Bible passage: Joshua 1:1–18
Session aim: To remember that God will be with us wherever we go

Theme introduction

Let people, especially children, say who they would like to have with them all the time and why. Comment that having God with us is better, in reality, than having the strongest, most powerful or kindest person in all the world. Refer to the story of Joshua, in which the children will be discovering that God promised him, 'I will always be with you'. Joshua had a tough time ahead. God did not take the trouble away but he gave him the strength to deal with whatever happened!

Wherever we go, God is with us. He never leaves us. Two people could read this adapted part of Psalm 139 below, or you could read it all together using the PowerPoint web download **web ref AASA3.starters_12**.

Lord God, you are everywhere.
If I fly high into the sky, towards the rising sun,
Lord God, you are there.
If I lose my way and all direction,
Lord God, you are there.
If I hide in the dark, full of fear or shame,
Lord God, you are there.
You are in the light and the dark, the day and the night.

You notice everywhere I go.
Lord God, you are there.
You hear every word I speak.
Lord God, you are there.
I cannot hide from you.
Lord God, you are everywhere.
You know right from wrong, those who love you and those who don't.

Lord God, you are everywhere.
You know me inside out, upside down, through and through,
And you love me!

Song suggestions

'As we are gathered'	ts 29
'Be still and know'	ts 48
'Come down, O love divine'	SOF 1202
'Do not be afraid'	SOF 1213
'Be bold, be strong'	JP 14
'I am with you'	BSBS

Prayer idea

If you have a weekly news sheet outlining events in the coming week, suggest that people use it as a prayer prompt. They can pray daily for the church's activities, those planning and running events, and all the people involved. It would be especially good this week to pray that everyone will know that, wherever they go, God is with them.

Extra idea

At the start of the series on Joshua, it would be valuable for everyone to learn the *Learn and remember* verse of Joshua 1:9b. You could sing the song 'I am with you' based on the verse, from *Bitesize Bible Songs*, or divide the verse into four sections, facing north, south, east and west as you say each part.

You could listen to this story from *The Big Bible Storybook* audio book, 'Joshua leads God's people'.

Help for the spies

Bible passage: Joshua 2:1–24
Session aim: To recognise that God has the power to keep his people safe

Theme introduction

To introduce the idea of having the power to protect, talk about local or national schemes which are protecting wildlife (for example, in the UK, The Woodland Trust or The Wildlife Trusts). Display photographs, if possible, and briefly outline how people are saving animals and plants from danger. Point out that only people have the power to protect – the animals and plants, wonderful though they are, cannot do it for themselves. The dangers that surround them are too great. They need people's care, knowledge and power.

Draw parallels with the way God protects us. Just like our wildlife, we are unaware of many of the dangers that surround us and we are much more vulnerable than we think! Encourage the congregation to think of ways in which we are able to protect ourselves. Conclude that, although there are lots of ways in which we *can* protect ourselves, only God has the love, knowledge and power to keep us safe in ways we can only begin to imagine.

The children will be hearing how God protected his people from danger, as Joshua led the people into the Promised Land.

Song suggestions

'Father, I place into your hands'	ts 97
'In heav'nly armour'	ts 228
'Jesus, you're my firm foundation'	ts 302
'Lead us, heavenly Father'	SOF 1412
'Our God is strong and mighty'	SOF 1496
'I am with you'	BSBS

Prayer idea

Find out about a church, perhaps of your own denomination or in your local area, which is in danger. The danger might be due to natural forces, a political situation, difficult circumstances or persecution.

Small cards or bookmarks could be made so that the congregation can pray for God's protection for this fellowship throughout the week.

Extra idea

Select verses from Psalm 91 and use them as a responsive reading. After each verse, the congregation should respond: **You are my God and I will trust you.** A version ready for use can be downloaded from **web ref AASA3. starters_13**.

The LORD is my fortress
Live under the protection of God Most High
and stay in the shadow of God All-Powerful.
You are my God and I will trust you.
Then you will say to the LORD,
"You are my fortress, my place of safety;
you are my God, and I trust you."
You are my God and I will trust you.
The LORD will keep you safe
from secret traps and deadly diseases.
You are my God and I will trust you.
He will spread his wings over you
and keep you secure.
You are my God and I will trust you.
The LORD Most High is your fortress.
Run to him for safety.
You are my God and I will trust you.
God will command his angels
to protect you wherever you go.
You are my God and I will trust you.
The LORD says,
"If you love me and truly know who I am,
I will rescue you and keep you safe.
You are my God and I will trust you.
When you are in trouble, call out to me.
I will answer and be there
to protect and honour you.
You are my God and I will trust you.
You will live a long life
and see my saving power."
You are my God and I will trust you.

River crossing

Bible passage: Joshua 3:1–17
Session aim: To see that, with God's power, anything is possible

Theme introduction

Display a series of items that have the power to do something practical and useful (a tool, a torch, an item of protective clothing, something used in cookery and so on). Ask if anyone can see what these things have in common. When the congregation has guessed the connection, or when you have revealed it, say that there is another connection. The power of each item is limited. For example, a torch has the power to help us see when it is dark, but is no use when making cakes; a helmet has the power to protect our heads, but cannot saw wood. The items only have power when used for the proper purpose.

Together, make a list of the ways we see God's power in our own lives – in creation, healing, changing us and so on. Notice that there is nothing bad on the list. God's power only does good things! That is because God loves us and wants the best for us. It is true to say that, with God's power, anything is possible. The children will be exploring how God's power enabled his people to cross the River Jordan.

Song suggestions

'God of glory'	ts 130
'Mighty is our God'	ts 357
'Our God is so great'	ts 420
'My God is so big'	JP 169
'Our God is strong and mighty'	SOF 1496
'I am with you'	BSBS

Prayer idea

Lead the following prayer. The leader should say the lines marked 'A', after which the whole congregation responds with 'B' and a small group of speakers with line 'C'.

A   When bad things happen in our world...
B   **God of power, help us.**
C   *There is nothing your power cannot do.*
A   When we face bullies or people who try to hurt us in any way…
B   **God of power, help us.**
C   *There is nothing your power cannot do.*
A   When we face problems and challenges that seem too big to handle…
B   **God of power, help us.**
C   *There is nothing your power cannot do.*
A   When everything seems against us…
B   **God of power, help us.**
C   *There is nothing your power cannot do.*

Extra idea

As a way of praying for others, take a topical item in which people seem in an impossible situation. If possible, display some visual evidence of this situation. Ask everyone to imagine this as a river in flood, impossible to cross. With God's power, anything is possible; so imagine the water being pushed back as in Joshua 3. Thank God for his power!

You could listen to this story from *The Big Bible Storybook* audio book, 'Over the river'.

The all-age service in this book on page 97 explores the second part of this story in Joshua 4.

Walls fall

Bible passage: Joshua 6:1–27
Session aim: To recognise that God is victorious

Theme introduction

Challenge someone to a simple game (preferably something that can be seen by everyone – like a large version of Connect 4 or Jenga). Make the game as dramatic as possible, with different parts of the congregation cheering each player. Declare the winner and encourage cheers and clapping!

Although winning a game can seem like a great victory, it is nothing like as inspiring as the great victory won by Joshua which the children will explore in this service.

God was taking his people into the land he had promised and there was marching, trumpets sounding and cheering (everyone can produce suitable sound effects). God won the battle for his people! (Great cheers and celebration!)

Explain that God is victorious in everything he does. Joshua listened to God and obeyed him. If he had gone his own way, Joshua would not have seen a victory.

Song suggestions

'He that is in us'	ts 167
'Our God is awesome in power'	ts 419
'We want to see Jesus lifted high'	ts 559
'Who is on the Lord's side?'	SOF 610
'Let God arise'	SOF 309
'I am with you'	BBS

Prayer idea

Prepare a large board with a brick-shaped piece of paper at the centre. Write 'God is victorious' in large letters on the shape. Give out smaller pieces of paper in the same shape. Allow time for people to write or draw a situation in which they would like to see God's victory. These can be formed into a wall by placing them around the words 'God is victorious' as a prayerful act.

Extra idea

Orchestrate a triumphant ending to 'The Lord's Prayer'. The majority of the prayer should be said quietly and reverently as a way of listening to what God wants from us. The ending should be said loudly or even shouted to emphasise the words 'kingdom', 'power' and 'glory'. Percussion instruments could be played, arms waved or hands clapped. Provide a visual display of 'The Lord's Prayer', since there are several versions and lots of people, even in churches, do not know it by heart.

You could listen to this story from *The Big Bible Storybook* audio book, 'The walls of Jericho'.

Only Jesus

Find out what Jesus said about himself and discover that he is the only one to follow.

Learn and remember verse:
*'Jesus [said], "I am the way, the truth, and the life;
no one goes to the Father except by me."' John 14:6*

The song, 'The way', from *Bitesize Bible Songs* puts these words to music and can be downloaded from www.scriptureunion.org.uk/light. Additional ideas for learning this verse can be found on **web ref AASA3.starters_11**.

The all-age service outline that is part of this series is 'So, who is Jesus? on page 101, focusing on John 6:1–15; Acts 1:1–11; with an optional reading, Exodus 16:13–18.

The only way

Bible passage: John 14:1–14
Session aim: To discover that Jesus is the way to know God

April – June
6

Theme introduction

Invite two people to tell everyone, briefly, how they first became Christians. Choose people with contrasting stories: perhaps a lifelong follower and a sudden convert; someone who heard about Jesus at an evangelistic rally, and someone who heard about him from a close friend. Bring out the common factor in these varying tales: Jesus is the way to know God.

Song suggestions

'Deep love'	*LFE*
'Anyone can come to God'	*RU*
'The way'	*BSBS*
'Jesus is the password'	*ks 202*
'Jesus, be the centre'	*ks 587*
'Jesus is greater'	*ks 196*
'Jesus is the name we honour'	*SOF 870*

Prayer idea

Pray that, as you share your lives together as a church, you will become more like Jesus. All join in the response, speaking firmly and clearly as you declare your agreement. This is also available as a PowerPoint download at **web ref AASA3. starters_14**.

Lord God, may this church be full of kindness and compassion.
So that all may give glory to God,
Make us more like Jesus.

May this church be humble, looking out for one another's interests.

So that all may give glory to God,
Make us more like Jesus.

May this church be willing and able to obey God's purpose.
So that all may give glory to God,
Make us more like Jesus.

May this church hold out a message of life.
So that all may give glory to God,
Make us more like Jesus.

May this church be glad and full of joy.
So that all may give glory to God,
Make us more like Jesus.
(From *A Church for All Ages*, Peter Graystone and Eileen Turner, Scripture Union 1993)

Extra idea

The *Learn and remember* verse is John 14:6. Jesus said, 'I am the way, the truth, and the life; no one goes to the Father except by me.' Play the audio track of 'The way' from *Bitesize Bible Songs* and watch the PowerPoint (or look at a poster of the words). Repeat the audio and all join in with singing the song and learning the Bible verse.

The last weekend in May 2009 was the first National Family Week. Visit www.nationalfamilyweek.co.uk to find out what is happening in 2010. How could your church celebrate families this year? How about combining a family event with Pentecost on 23 May? For more details of Scripture Union's families' ministry, visit www.scriptureunion.org.uk/families.

Staying close

Bible passage: John 15:1–17
Session aim: To discover that we can only live as Jesus wants us to if we are close to him

Theme introduction

Describe the work of Karl Barth (go to Google Images for photos), a great twentieth-century theologian. A photo of him is available from **web ref AASA3.starters_15**. Barth (1886–1968) published more than five hundred articles and books, taught in universities and debated with the greatest thinkers of the age. His four volume *Church Dogmatics* is more than 6 million words long!

A student asked if he could sum up what was most important about his life's work and theology. Barth responded quickly: 'Yes, in the words of a song my mother used to sing to me, "Jesus loves me, this I know, for the Bible tells me so."'

Song suggestions

'Call to me'	LFE
'God's promises'	LFE
'I try to do what's good'	RU
'Can we love one another?'	ks 22
'God loves you'	ks 80
'Jesus, send me the helper'	ks 213
'The way'	BSBS

Prayer idea

Before you pray, stand to practise these actions together. First, use both hands to point in front of you; then put your hands behind you; next put your hands to your sides; and finally wrap your arms around yourself in a hug. Lead this prayer, allowing enough time to do the actions.

Jesus is before us,
Preparing the way.
(Point both hands in front of you.)
Jesus is behind us,
Helping us, come what may.
(Put both hands behind you.)
Jesus is beside us,
He's here with us today.
(Put both hands by your sides.)
Jesus is always with us,

Every hour of every day.
(Give yourself a hug.)
Jesus says to us: 'I call you friends, because I have told you everything I have heard from my Father.' (John 15:15b).

Repeat the prayer words and actions.

Extra idea

The *Learn and remember* verse is John 14:6. Jesus said, 'I am the way, the truth, and the life; no one goes to the Father except by me.' Show the lyrics of 'The way' from *Bitesize Bible Songs* and read them together, while a musician plays the tune from the sheet music. Repeat the music and, this time, join in with singing.

Read or tell Oscar Wilde's fable of 'The Happy Prince', available in many print and audio versions; the story words are available if you put the title into a search engine. This is a story which speaks for itself – and which can be enjoyed by children as young as five.

Don't forget National Family Week at the end of May and the opportunities it may present!

Another helper

Bible passage: John 14:15–31; 16:5–15
Session aim: To find out how the Holy Spirit helps us

Theme introduction

Borrow an idea from Corrie ten Boom. Pull on a glove and explain: 'I have a glove here on my hand. The glove cannot do anything by itself but, when my hand is in it, it can do many things. True, it is not the glove, but my hand in the glove that acts.'

If today is the Day of Pentecost, you can celebrate the coming of the Holy Spirit. Wiggle your gloved hand and say: 'We are gloves. It is the Holy Spirit in us who is the hand, who does the job. We have to make room for the hand so that every finger is filled.'

Song suggestions

'Love, joy, peace'	LFE
'Because of who he is'	ks 18
'Hang on, stand still'	ks 94
'Holy Spirit, fill me now'	ks 514
'Father God, we worship you'	SOF 93
'The Spirit lives to set us free'	SOF 1555
'The way'	BSBS

Prayer idea

Divide the congregation into two groups, to say alternate lines. All say the final two lines. Repeat with different groupings. Try, for example: worship leader/congregation; younger people/older people; male/female; front rows/back rows.

Where the Spirit of the Lord is,
There is love for one another.
Where the Spirit of the Lord is,
There is power to make our faith strong.
Where the Spirit of the Lord is,
There is joy that's more than words can say.
Where the Spirit of the Lord is,
There is freedom in God's family.
Where the Spirit of the Lord is,
There is sharing of the good news.
Set us on fire in the service of God,
Fill us, Lord God, with your Spirit.
(From *A Church for All Ages*, Peter Graystone and Eileen Turner, Scripture Union 1993)

Extra idea

Develop this idea of feather prayers. Talk about the Holy Spirit being like the breath of God who helps us when we pray. Give each person a feather to hold. (Buy a bag of mixed colours from a craft shop.) What does it feel like? What is it like to stroke? What is it like to rub gently against our hands? Invite the congregation to see how far they can blow their feathers.

Pause and chat in small groups about things and people that you want to tell God about. Play with the feathers again and, this time, call out the prayer ideas as you blow the feathers.

You could listen to the story of Pentecost from *The Big Bible Storybook* audio book, 'Early one morning'.

Praise the Lord

Bible passage: Psalm 150:1–6
Session aim: To enjoy using music to praise God

Theme introduction

As the service begins, play some energetic and joyful music (the worship group can play, or you can use a CD). Comment on how exuberant it was. Then get ready to praise God with your own musical instruments. Set some ground rules before you start: for example, instruments are to be placed on the floor when not in use; when you lift your hand, it means 'stop'.

Give out any percussion instruments (shakers, bells, rhythm sticks) you have available or practise clapping, imitating trumpets, or tapping your feet. Make sure adults have instruments as well as children. Why are you doing this? Because today's Bible passage is all about praising God – noisily! Play the instruments during your songs today – and have at least one verse which is instruments-only.

Song suggestions

'So amazing God'	LFE
'Wow!'	RU
'The way'	BSBS
'God is good, God is great'	ks 73
'What noise shall we make?'	ks 369
'Let's sing'	ks 228
'Lord, you gave me joy'	ks 242
'Praise him on the trumpet'	SOF 464
'God is our Father'	SOF 134
'Give thanks to the Lord'	SOF 1241
'In your presence'	SOF 1356

Lots of songs are included for this session to give you plenty of opportunity to praise God together with music.

Prayer idea

Practise a Mexican wave. Begin with everyone sitting down. Begin the wave in one area of the group. One person should stand up (or raise their hands). As soon as they do so, the person next to them should stand (or raise their hands). The effect then passes round the whole group.

Use the wave as a way of saying 'Amen'. To work effectively, everyone needs to watch what is happening so they know when to move. (It is easier for children when they are sitting in a circle, rather than in rows.) Keep it light-hearted: half the fun of a Mexican wave is when it gets muddled up!

Lead the prayers, thanking, praising and asking God. At the end of each short prayer, everyone can join in the Mexican wave to show that they are saying that prayer too.

Extra idea

Invite everyone to bring any musical instrument that they play, however well or badly, to the service. Assemble a scratch orchestra to accompany the singing for this service, although if there has been time to practise, the quality of the sound will be improved. This might also be an opportunity to spot future musical talent. Make a point of thanking the regular musicians who often give of their time and talent with little recognition.

You could listen to a reworking of Psalm 150 from *The Big Bible Storybook* audio book, 'Praise God'.

In the UK, the public exam season is well under way. Search www.schoolslive.org for advice on how to help children and young people in your church who are taking school exams at this time of year. Have a supply of *Exam Stress (And How to Beat It!)* leaflets, produced by Childline. Call 020 7650 3444 or email info@childline.org.uk. Include the Childline helpline number on your church notices (UK only).

Jesus the healer

Jesus demonstrates his love and compassion as he meets the needs of people he encounters.

Learn and remember verse:
'Let us keep our eyes fixed on Jesus, on whom our faith depends from beginning to end.' Hebrews 12:2

The song 'Eyes fixed', from *Bitesize Bible Songs,* puts these words to music and can be downloaded from www.scriptureunion.org.uk/light. Additional ideas for learning this verse can be found on **web ref AASA3.starters_11**.

The all-age service outline that is part of this series is 'Jesus' love goes on and on and...' on page 105, focusing on Mark 5:24b–34; Isaiah 41:17–20.

Many healed

Bible passage: Mark 1:29–39
Session aim: To learn that Jesus shows his care by healing people

April – June

10

Theme introduction

Have someone introduce today's theme by saying, 'Let me tell you about my mother-in-law…' Build this up as though they are going to tell a string of caustic jokes – but then go against the stereotype by giving warm and genuine praise to a lovely member of the family. (If she happens to be a member of your congregation, how about surprising her with a bouquet or a box of chocolates?)

Describe how Peter's mother-in-law was at the heart of his family and his home. So when she was ill, everyone would have been affected. Introduce Jesus, not coming with flowers or chocolates, but with something even better…

Song suggestions

'God is an awesome God'	*LFE*
'Eyes fixed'	*BSBS*
'Who spoke words'	*ks 387*
'I reach up high'	*SOF 1358*
'Jesus is the name we honour'	*SOF 870*
'Jesus, Jesus, Healer, Saviour'	*SOF 1388*

Prayer idea

Talk about God's promises and how he cares for people. Explain that you are going to make a tree as a way of asking God to help people who are not well. Set up a twiggy branch in a steady container, or use a real tree outside. Give each person a paper leaf shape (or luggage label, or a length of ribbon or other fabric) and invite them to fix their leaf on the tree with string or sticky tape, as they pray for people who need God to make them well. (They could write or draw on the leaves, too.)

Assure everyone that God cares about each person represented by the prayer leaves. Add to the prayer tree over the next three sessions. Make sure you add extra leaves when you hear of answers to your prayers.

Extra idea

The *Learn and remember* verse is Hebrews 12:2, 'Let us keep our eyes fixed on Jesus, on whom our faith depends from beginning to end.' Play the audio track of 'Eyes fixed' from *Bitesize Bible Songs* and watch the PowerPoint (or look at a poster of the words). Repeat the audio and all join in with singing the song and learning the Bible verse.

You could listen to the story of Peter's mother-in-law from *The Big Bible Storybook* audio book, 'At Peter's house'.

This weekend is the World Weekend of Prayer for Children at Risk. It would be a natural development of this session's theme to pray for all children in need because Jesus cares for them. For more details visit www.viva.org.

A man asks for help

Bible passage: Mark 1:40–45

Session aim: To hear that Jesus wants to make people well

Theme introduction

Conduct a survey of your congregation. Make it as light-hearted as possible, but be aware that some people might be embarrassed or not wish to join in, so respect their feelings. Say that you are going to ask a few questions, and suggest people indicate if their answer is 'yes' by raising a hand, standing or shouting 'yes'.

Ask: Have you ever…
- been ill
- known someone who was ill
- helped someone who was ill
- been helped when you were ill
- prayed for someone who was ill
- prayed for yourself when you were ill
- had someone else praying for you when you were ill?

Ask: Do you think…
- Jesus can heal people
- you have been healed by Jesus
- Jesus wants people to be well?

Introduce a member of the congregation who can tell a true story about their own healing experience. It need not be spectacular but choose someone who can speak genuinely and who is confident that God was responsible for the recovery.

Song suggestions

'Who was the man?'	*LFE*
'Eyes fixed'	*BSBS*
'Jesus' hands were kind hands'	*ks 194*
'Jesus' love is very wonderful'	*ks 208*
'Who spoke words of wisdom?'	*ks 387*
'Jesus never, never'	*ks 602*
'Lord of all hopefulness'	*SOF 902*

Prayer idea

Talk about asking God for help (as the man does in today's Bible reading). Remind everyone about your prayer tree (from the last session) and spend a few minutes sharing any answers to prayers. Add the answers to the tree, on different coloured paper leaves.

Give each person a paper leaf shape (or label or ribbon) and invite them to fix their leaf on the tree, with string or sticky tape, as they ask God for help. (They could write or draw on the leaves, too.) You will be using the prayer tree again next time, so encourage everyone to look forward to further answers.

Extra idea

To help everyone engage with this story, you could read Mark 1:40–45 in a dramatic way, giving a small group of people four actions to perform as the story is told. Each action has to do with communicating by speech: begging, speaking with compassion, warning and gossiping everywhere.

You could listen to the story of this man whom Jesus healed from *The Big Bible Storybook* audio book, 'A man with leprosy'.

Healing on the Sabbath

Bible passage: Mark 3:1–6
Session aim: To realise that not everyone liked the things Jesus did

Theme introduction

Ask a few people (choose those with a good sense of humour!) to help you with an experiment. You have a number of everyday tasks for them to perform – but they can only use one hand and are not to help each other. How easy is it to tie a shoelace? Sharpen a pencil and write a note? Find a Bible reference? Wrap something in cling film? Encourage your volunteers with plenty of clapping and cheering.

Thank them for their efforts and interview them briefly about these 'easy' tasks. What was it like? Were they able to work out ways of getting the task done? (Aim to show life is more awkward when you cannot use your hands freely, but avoid too much analysis.)

Song suggestions

'All the time'	*RU*
'Eyes fixed'	*BSBS*
'Jesus, never, never'	*ks 602*
'Hands, hands, fingers, thumbs'	*ks 93*
'I believe in Jesus'	*ks 122*
'Touch a finger'	*ks 744*
'King of kings'	*SOF 1404*

Prayer idea

Comment that there were people who did not like what Jesus did and ultimately they plotted to kill him. Acknowledge that there may be people or organisations in your locality who may object to what churches are seeking to do in reaching out to others. As appropriate, pray that God will step in to remove the obstacles that are being put in front of you. You could add these prayers to the prayer tree.

Begin by all praying with your hands covering your eyes as an obstacle to seeing clearly. Tell God about these situations and ask him to act. Conclude by thanking God that his power is so great that he can overcome any obstacle and nothing can separate us from God's love. Everyone should remove their hands as you read Romans 8:31,37–39 as a reminder of God's power.

Extra idea

Display photos and information about your mission partners and pray for them in the light of this theme, that even though they will encounter opposition, God is on their side.

You could listen to the story of the man whom Jesus healed from *The Big Bible Storybook* audio book, 'A man with a damaged hand'.

A dead girl lives!

Bible reading: Mark 5:21–43
Session aim: To realise that Jesus showed his compassion in surprising ways

Theme introduction

Here's a real story from the *Light* editorial team. A children's group leader wrote to say the children in her group had listened carefully as she told the story of Jesus bringing Jairus' daughter back to life. She then asked them, as the *Splash!* activity suggested, what they would like Jesus to do for them. She later wrote to say, 'A seven-year-old in my group logically reached the conclusion that it was possible to ask that Jesus might bring his grandad back to life. Help! What would you say?'

What would *you* say? Let the congregation discuss this in small groups for a few minutes; then ask them to share their ideas.
(The *Splash!* editor's answer can be found on **web ref AASA3.starters_16** .

Song suggestions

'Who was the man?'	*LFE*
'God is an awesome God'	*LFE*
'Eyes fixed'	*BSBS*
'Jesus is greater'	*ks* 196
'My Jesus, my Saviour'	*ks* 257
'Jesus put this song'	*SOF* 299
'Your love is amazing'	*SOF* 1676

Prayer idea

Is your prayer tree full yet? Enjoy the answers you have received. Have all the prayers been answered yet? Are there new prayers that people want to add to the tree? Jairus asked Jesus to make his daughter better but, for a while, it seemed as if it was too late for Jesus to help. Then Jesus said something wonderful to Jairus: 'Don't be afraid, only believe.' Jairus did – and so can we!

Celebrate the answers to prayer – but *don't be afraid* to add new prayers. God is kind and concerned for all our needs: *only believe.*

Extra idea

After reading the story, either produce this wordsearch on a flip chart or download it from **web ref AASA3.starters_17**. Ask the following questions, which are in chronological order. When the answer has been given, see if you can find that word in the wordsearch.

+	D	E	S	I	O	N
J	A	I	R	U	S	H
P	U	F	E	E	T	A
E	G	T	N	F	W	N
E	H	H	R	O	E	D
L	T	R	U	O	L	E
S	E	E	O	D	V	I
A	R	E	M	+	E	D

Who came to see Jesus in the story?	JAIRUS
Who in his family was ill?	DAUGHTER
What part of Jesus' body did he fall at?	FEET
What did he think his daughter would do?	DIE
How many of Jesus' friends went with him?	THREE
Who greeted Jesus at the house?	MOURNERS
What were they making?	NOISE
Jesus said that the girl was not dead but…	ASLEEP
How old was the girl?	TWELVE
What did Jesus take hold of?	HAND
What did Jesus say her parents should give her?	FOOD

You could listen to the story of the girl who Jesus brought back to life from 'Too late!', the audio Bible story from *Listen with the Bible* (CD2) or from *The Big Bible Storybook* audio book, 'Jairus and his daughter'.

Judges rule God's people

This series explores how God gave power to his chosen people and how they responded.

Learn and remember verse:
'I know, LORD, that you are all-powerful;
that you can do everything you want.' Job 42:2

The song 'Everything you want', from *Bitesize Bible Songs 2,* puts these words to music and can be downloaded from www.scriptureunion.org.uk/light. Additional ideas for learning this verse can be found on **web ref AASA3.starters_11**.

The all-age service outline that is part of this series is 'Take that!' on page 109, focusing on Judges 3:12–30 and Luke 5:1–11.

Power to the leaders

Bible passage: Judges 4:1–24
Session aim: To realise that God equips some people to be leaders

July – Sept

1

Theme introduction

Explain that you have been thinking about a particular person and you are going to play a quiz to see if everyone else can work out the identity of this mystery person (Deborah.). You could run this quite simply, or make it a glitzy event with spotlights, sound effects and sequins!

Give out clues in the following order such as: a politician; a wartime leader; a prophet; a general; a singer; a legal expert; a woman; lived in the Old Testament; told Barak what to do… Once the character has been guessed, challenge people to find verses in Judges 4 and 5 which show the characteristics you have mentioned.

Song suggestions

'Twisting back in time'	LFE
'Wow!'	RU
'Everything you want'	BSBS2
'Great big God'	GBG
'When a knight won his spurs'	ks 371
'Be bold'	SOF 37
'He who would valiant be'	SOF 174

Prayer idea

Pray for leaders at all levels of society: nationally, internationally, and locally. Mention specific issues that are in the news where leaders need God's wisdom to know and do the right thing.

Pray for leaders in your church: those who lead worship, who preach, who teach others, who lead home groups and groups for children and young

people. Invite members of those groups to name their leaders aloud and to thank God for them.

Extra idea

The *Learn and remember* verse is Job 42:2: 'I know, LORD, that you are all-powerful; that you can do everything you want.' Before the service, print off multiple copies of the words of the verse (use the 'poster' option on *Bitesize Bible Songs 2* for the song 'Everything you want'); cut each copy of the verse into four pieces and spread the pieces around your meeting area. During the service, set the task for the congregation to find four pieces and put them together to find the Bible verse (perhaps working in small groups; alternatively, choose some children to do this). Read the words together – and then repeat, making sure your voices sound 'powerful'!

You could listen to the story of Deborah from *The Big Bible Storybook* audio book, 'Deborah'.

The book, *A tent peg, a jawbone and a sheepskin rug* (SU) written by Malc Halliday and illustrated by Ian Potter, tells the story of Deborah (and all the judges) in a compelling style. The sin cycle illustration from this book, which sums up the whole of Judges, can be found on **web ref AASA3.starters_18**. You could use this throughout the series. It runs like this:

Here we go, round the sin cycle again. Forget about God; it all goes wrong; wonder what to do; eventually remember God; repent; God puts it right; everyone is happy; until…

Power to the weak

Bible reading: Judges 6:11–16,33–40
Session aim: To understand that God gives courage

Theme introduction

Play a quiz based on *The Weakest Link*. Choose several volunteers as contestants, including one person who has been primed to lose every question. Ask several rounds of trivial and easy questions, with your stooge getting everything wrong. Then ask the contestants and the congregation to decide who has got the most wrong answers and is the 'weakest link'. Reverse the usual pattern of the quiz by sending the other contestants back to their places and rewarding the person who did not 'win'. When the 'viewers' object (have someone ready to comment, if this does not happen spontaneously), explain that in the Bible story that the children will explore, Gideon knew he was the weakest link – but he was the one whom God chose to be a leader.

Weakest link questions can be found on **web ref AASA3.starters_19**.

Song suggestions

'So cool'	RU
'Everything you want'	BSBS2
'God's people'	ks 86
'Be bold'	SOF 37
'My God is so big'	ks 255
'Great is he'	SOF 1254
'To him we come'	SOF 1569

Prayer idea

Gideon was weak and it was God who enabled him to become a successful leader. It was not Gideon's power or courage that made the difference.

Use the words of Psalm 99:1–5, as shown in the next column, to focus on God. Demonstrate and practise the actions first, and then invite everyone to join in the words of the psalm which can be projected (see **web ref AASA3.starters_20**) or everyone can echo each phrase after you.

Verse 1: raise both arms and point upwards
Verse 2: bring your arms down, in an arc, to your sides
Verse 3: cup your hands and hold them in front of you
Verse 4: clench your fists
Verse 5: stand, sit or kneel – however you prefer to pray.

Psalm 99:1–5
1. Our LORD, you are King!
You rule from your throne above the winged creatures,
as people tremble and the earth shakes.
2. You are praised in Zion,
and you control all nations.
3. Only you are God!
And your power alone,
so great and fearsome, is worthy of praise.
4. You are our mighty King, a lover of fairness,
who sees that justice is done everywhere in Israel.
5. Our LORD and our God,
we praise you and kneel down to worship you,
the God of holiness!

Extra idea

It would be appropriate to interview someone who has experienced being the odd one out or the one whom no one expected to excel in any way.

You could listen to the story of Gideon from *The Big Bible Storybook* audio book, 'God chooses Gideon'.

Power to the few

Bible reading: Judges 7:1–22
Session aim: To recognise that God gives power to those who trust and obey him

Theme introduction

Act out the final stage of a competition where the contestant, a military general, gets to choose the equipment for a battle. This 'general' will open boxes, one at a time, and read out the list inside.
Box 1: 'bow, arrow, catapult, ballista, trebuchet'.
Box 2: 'musket, cavalry, cannon'.
Box 3: 'tank, stealth bomber, machine gun'.
Which should the general choose? Ask the congregation to help him decide.
While he hesitates, bring forward Box 4: 'trumpets, lights and jars…' Turn the list over and read '… and God'.

Congratulate the general for choosing Box 4 but, as an aside to the audience, wonder whether he has done the right thing. Is a light really going to work better than a tank? By the end of today's service, the children should know the answer.

Song suggestions

'God's promises'	*LFE*
'Everything you want'	*BSBS2*
'Be bold'	*SOF 37*
'My God is so big'	*ks 255*
'For I'm building'	*SOF 111*
'In heavenly armour'	*SOF 237*
'We are marching'	*SOF 1076*

Prayer idea

Focus your prayers on areas of the world where there are wars and armed conflicts. At the time of writing, United Nations troops were involved in 15 peacekeeping operations around the world. http://en.wikipedia.org/wiki/Ongoing_conflicts gives an up-to-date map and lists of conflict areas in the world. Be sensitive as you invite your church to pray about these areas, and about current news items. You could use a large world map or a globe and mark each country where there is warfare – and each place you pray for.

Pray for those making political decisions, for those actively involved in conflict and for those affected directly and indirectly. Pray that those in positions of power and responsibility may grasp that God has put them there; pray that they will act accordingly – with wisdom.

Extra idea

Over the holiday time, many churches will be running different forms of outreach – holiday clubs, play schemes, holidays and camps, and children and young people may be going away to various Christian activities. Make sure that the whole church is involved in praying for these. Many people involved will feel in need of God's strength as they seek to obey him. For details of Scripture Union holidays and missions, visit www.scriptureunion.org.uk/holidays.

You could listen to the second part of the story of Gideon from *The Big Bible Storybook* audio book, 'Gideon listens to God'.

Power misused

Bible reading: Judges 13:1–7; 16:4–31
Session aim: To see that God gives strength to be used wisely

Theme introduction

Invite four extroverts to take part in your church's 'World's Strongest Person' competition. Some suggestions could be:

- Log lift: raise a twig above your head; repeat five times.
- Lorry pull: tie a piece of string to a model vehicle and pull it along.
- Fridge carry: carry a cool bag around the church.
- Atlas stones: in turn, lift a table tennis ball, a tennis ball, a football, and a large beach ball from the floor, and place them on a table.

Award points for style, speed and silliness. Be lavish with praise, points and prizes! Do any of your competitors feel ready to compete in the international World's Strongest Man event? Probably not! But there would have been a biblical contender and he could have won easily – any ideas who? (Samson.)

Song suggestions

'God's promises'	*LFE*
'Everything you want'	*BSBS2*
'God's people'	*ks 86*
'When a knight won his spurs'	*ks 371*
'He who would valiant be'	*SOF 174*
'We are marching'	*SOF 1076*
'Restore, O Lord'	*SOF 483*

Prayer idea

Samson did not use his strength wisely and turned away from God. But God did not leave him. God does not leave us, either, no matter how we fail or forget him.

Either read the poem 'Footprints' as a meditative prayer or listen to 'Footprints in the Sand' from the album *Spirit* by Leona Lewis.

Or invite everyone to sit quietly, with eyes closed.

- Clench your fists and think about the wrong things you have said or done. Pause for a few moments.
- Open your hands to show you are sorry. Pause again.
- Hold your hands upwards as you receive God's forgiveness.

Extra idea

A curious fact, from Tate and Lyle www.tateandlyle.com.

Abram Lyle had strong religious beliefs, which is why the Lyle's Golden Syrup trademark depicts a quotation from the Bible. In Judges 14, Samson was returning to the land of the Philistines to marry a wife, having seen a woman there that took his fancy. During the journey, he killed a lion, and, returning home past the same spot, he noticed that a swarm of bees had formed a comb of honey in the carcass. Samson later turned this into a riddle: Out of the eater came forth meat, and out of the strong came forth sweetness.

The 'lion and bees' quickly became identified with Lyle's Golden Syrup, and it was registered as Lyle's trademark in 1904. However, no one knows why Lyle chose the wording 'out of the strong came forth sweetness'. Was he referring to the tin holding the syrup – or the company producing it?

The famous Lyle's Golden Syrup tin is now one of the most familiar sights in British kitchens – and instantly recognisable among the 20,000 items stocked by today's supermarkets. The distinctive packaging has hardly changed since 1885 and, in 2007, it was named by Guinness World Records as the world's oldest branding!

Love stories

This series looks at stories that Jesus told that demonstrate God's love.

Learn and remember verse:
'Leave all your worries with him, because he cares for you.' 1 Peter 5:7

The song 'Leave all your worries', from *Bitesize Bible Songs,* puts these words to music and can be downloaded from www.scriptureunion.org.uk/light.

The all-age service outline that is part of this series is 'Lost property' on page 113, focusing on Deuteronomy 7:6−11 and Luke 15:1,2,8−10.

Who to love

Bible passage: Luke 10:25–37
Session aim: To explore how to love God and love others

Theme introduction

If possible, invite two fans of rival football teams to come dressed in their supporters' kit. Alternatively, use the kit or photographs of two such teams. Ask the congregation questions about the sides, such as which has won the most games recently, which is on the way up or down in the league, which team has the best players, managers and supporters and so on. You could have fun using (non-abusive!) chants in turn to see which is the best.

Explain that in Jesus' time, just as in ours, there were people who were in opposing teams. The teams we read about were far more serious than sports sides, though. As in some places in the world today, religious and racial differences meant that people would not mix or might actually try to hurt those they did not agree with. Jesus told a story that spoke right into this situation; it is a story about how to love God and other people, and the children will be hearing it in their groups.

Song suggestions

'Love the Lord your God'	BSBS
'When I needed a neighbour'	JP 275
'Leave all your worries'	BSBS
'A new commandment I give unto you'	SOF 22
'Father God, I wonder'	MP 128
'I love You, Lord'	MP 287

Prayer idea

In which ways can people be different from us? Ask for suggestions. Some answers might be: age, where they live, which school they go to, which department they work in, which team they support. Use these suggestions to ask God to bless people who are different from us.

For a more interactive prayer, invite everyone who supports a popular local football team to stand up and pray for those who support their rivals, using a prayer such as: 'God, we ask that you would show your love to people who support [that team].' Repeat this prayer with a series of 'differences' to include different people in the congregation, such as people who are under or over 30, people who go to primary or senior schools, or people who work in business or the public sector. Be careful when choosing differences, being especially sensitive not to aggravate any rivalries.

Extra idea

Pray for a current international situation where there are difficulties between two rival groups, for example conflict in the Middle East. Pray that God would help his people to love those who are not the same as them − even their enemies.

You could listen to the story of the good Samaritan from *The Big Bible Storybook* audio book, 'Jesus tells a story'.

Love's invitation refused

Bible reading: Luke 14:15–24
Session aim: To recognise that we need to accept God's invitation

Theme introduction

Give everyone a pen and some paper and invite them to quickly draw or write the food they would like to have at a feast. You could give these out as people arrive, and allow a few minutes at the start of the service to do this activity.

Collect all the ideas and read them out as if you are describing the menu at a feast. If you have a confident artist (or two), make this more visual by challenging them to draw dishes, as you describe them, on a long piece of lining paper. As you finish, comment that the Bible says that God's kingdom is like a feast to which everyone has been invited. The children are going to discover what that means.

Song suggestions

'Leave all your worries'	BSBS
'Come and join the celebration'	MP 83
'Heaven invites you to a party'	ks2 496
'Come on and celebrate'	SOF 73
'Come, now is the time'	SOF 1205

Prayer idea

God has invited and welcomed us into a relationship with him. After each of the statements based around 1 Peter 5:7 (the *Learn and remember* verse), verses from Isaiah 55, and Matthew 11:28, say together: **We accept your invitation.**

'Leave all your worries with him, because he cares for you.'
Help us to trust you to care for us. (Pause to talk with God about needs.)
We accept your invitation.

'Return to the LORD our God. He will be merciful and forgive your sins.'
We pray that you will encourage us to ask you to forgive us for our sins, and that you will help us to accept your forgiveness. (Pause to identify any wrongdoing and ask for forgiveness.)
We accept your invitation.

'Listen carefully to me, and you will enjoy the very best foods.'
Help us to listen to you, and not to fill our minds with so many distractions. (Pause to listen and be still.)
We accept your invitation.

'If you are tired from carrying heavy burdens, come to me and I will give you rest.'
Help us to allow you to take the weight of all that troubles us, so that we can rest. (Pause for people to talk with God about what is burdening them.)
We accept your invitation.

Alternatively, these invitations could be printed and put in separate envelopes. Everyone should get into smaller groups, and a copy of each invitation should be given to each of the groups. Four people could be selected to read the prayers, whilst everyone else responds. These invitations are available as a download **web ref AASA3.starters_21**.

Extra idea

Pray for events such as holidays, holiday clubs or missions that people in your church are involved with. Ask the congregation for ideas and note them down. Blow up three balloons and write these words on them: 'Keep them safe', 'Give them lots of fun' and 'Help them know you better'. Play some music and bop the balloons around the congregation. When the music stops, start a prayer for one of the holidays or missions; then ask the people with the three balloons to say the prayer on their balloon. Repeat this for each of the ideas given, grouping some of them if you need to save time.

You could listen to the story of the great feast from *The Big Bible Storybook* audio book, 'Come to the party'.

Love for the lost

Bible reading: Luke 15:1–7
Session aim: To recognise how much God loves us

Theme introduction

Read to the congregation the story 'Guess how much I love you' by Sam McBratney. It's about a baby rabbit talking with his father about how much they love each other. Play a game of 'Hangman' to find out how we know that God loves us. Use this sentence from John 3:16 in the Good News Bible. (They are also the words to the song 'So much', available on the album *Bitesize Bible songs 2* and also as a download from www.scriptureunion.org.uk/music)

'God loved the world so much that he gave his only Son, so that everyone who believes in him may not die but have eternal life.'

When you have finished the game, recap that we know how much God loves us because he sent Jesus, his Son, to die for us so that we could be friends with God.

Alternatively, a group of people at the front of the meeting area could each invent an action for part of the verse to help people remember it.

Song suggestions

'So much'	*BSBS*
'Now and forever'	*LFE*
'Leave all your worries'	*BSBS*
'When I was lost you came and rescued me'	*SOF 1607*
'Love divine'	*SOF 377*

Prayer idea

If you have a lost property box, show it to everyone or borrow one from a children's group or a club run by your church. Ask some people to look at the things people have lost, and see if you can find any rightful owners. Say that sometimes when we lose things, we don't even realise they are lost; but when **we** get lost and go far away from God, he always knows and wants us to be 'found' by him. Give thanks to God that he looks for us and finds us. He always knows where we are.

Extra idea

Watch the scene from *Finding Nemo* when Nemo is finally found by his dad or play the song: 'Pretty Amazing Grace' by Neil Diamond. It's a grateful song all about God's love with the refrain 'pretty amazing'.

You could listen to this story from *The Big Bible Storybook* audio book, 'The lost sheep'.

How do you use the Bible within your all-age services? These three *Top Tips* titles will broaden your expectations of how to use the Bible and give you lots of practical ideas.

Sharing Bible stories
978 1 84427 328 7

Discovering the Bible with children
978 1 84427 335 5

Exploring the Bible with young people
978 1 84427 336 2

For more details go to
www.scriptureunion.org.uk/shop

Love that forgives

Bible reading: Luke 15:11–32
Session aim: To know that God loves us and will forgive us

Theme introduction

Ask someone to prepare to share a short story about a time when they were lost, or had lost something. Encourage them to share how they felt during the experience and afterwards, and what they did when they were found, or had found what they had lost.

Explain that Jesus told three stories about things that were lost. Ask if people can remember what they were. Explain that at the end of each of Jesus' stories, there was a party, to celebrate what had been found. Jesus said that the angels in heaven have a party each time a lost person is 'found' by God – that is, when someone chooses to follow God's way instead of their own. Follow this with an appropriate song or prayer to celebrate God's love.

Song suggestions

'So much'	BSBS2
'Leave all your worries'	BSBS
'I'm special'	JP 106
'I'm accepted, I'm forgiven'	MP 321
'When I was lost you came and rescued me'	SOF 1607

Prayer idea

Say this prayer of confession, inviting the congregation to say the response:
Thank you, God, that you love us and will forgive us.

Father God, we know you are love but we don't always *do* loving things. Sometimes we do unkind things to other people. Please forgive us.
Thank you, God, that you love us and will forgive us.

Lord Jesus, we know that you are love, but we don't always *say* loving things. Sometimes we say hurtful things to other people. Please forgive us.
Thank you, God, that you love us and will forgive us.

Holy Spirit, we know that you are love but we don't always *think* loving things. Sometimes we think nasty things about other people. Please forgive us.
Thank you, God, that you love us and will forgive us.

Thank you that because of Jesus, you forgive us, and we can be your friends. Amen

Extra idea

The *Learn and remember* verse is 1 Peter 1:7. 'Leave all your worries with him, because he cares for you.' Before the service, put the individual words on a set of cards and hide them around the building. Then say that you wanted to learn the verse together, but you've lost the cards with the words on them. Everyone should search for the cards; then the volunteers who find them should hold them up, standing in the right order for everyone to read them. Each time the verse is read, ask two or more volunteers to take away their card until everyone can say the verse without the cards.

You could listen to this story from *The Big Bible Storybook* audio book, 'A loving father'.

Responding to love

Bible reading: Psalm 25:1–22
Session aim: To see how we can pray to God who loves us

Theme introduction

Have fun with a Bible quiz about prayer. Split the congregation into two teams. When one team gets an answer right, give them a point or a turn at a game just for pairs. Score the points in a fun way. For scoring ideas, see *Ultimate Quizzes* (SU) by Richard and Mary Chewter.

Some suggested questions are below, and more can be found on **web ref AASA3.starters_22**:

Who laughed while he was talking with God? Abraham (Genesis 17:17).
Who asked God to rescue him from his brother? Jacob (Genesis 32:11).
Who told God he was worried no one would listen to him? Moses (Exodus 4:1).
Who cried and prayed silently for God to give her a child? Hannah (1 Samuel 1:9–12).
Who asked God to make the king say 'yes' to his request? Nehemiah (Nehemiah 1:11).
Who got in trouble for praying three times a day? Daniel (Daniel 6:10).

Song suggestions

'Trust in the Lord'	*BSBS*
'Call to me'	*BSBS2*
'Teach me your ways'	*ts 470*
'What a friend we have'	*MP 746*
'What a friend I've found'	*SOF 1109*
'Faithful one, so unchanging'	*SOF 89*
'Show me your ways'	*SOF 2023*

Prayer idea

Write a prayer together based on Psalm 25. In advance, write or print the following words from the psalm (taken from the Contemporary English Version) on Post-it notes and stick them randomly on flip chart paper under the following category headings:

God please... show, teach, guide, rescue, protect, forgive, remember, forget, lead, have pity, keep safe, see my troubles, show care
You are... patient, kind, honest, merciful, faithful
We... trust you; always look to you; come to you for shelter; obey you

Write your prayer on another flip chart or board, starting with 'God please...' and asking for people to suggest a word from the relevant Post-it notes, adding specifics such as 'God please guide us to live your way.' Start the next line with 'You are...' and the third with 'We...', adding appropriate suggestions. If you run out of words, encourage people to make their own suggestions. When the prayer seems complete, say it out loud together; end with 'Amen'.

Extra idea

Pray for children, parents and teachers starting the new term. Ask them to stand up, and invite people sitting near them to pray for them. Pray for the new term to be a good one for people; for those starting at new schools to be confident, knowing that God is with them.

Sharing the good news

This series explores the effect that the good news of Jesus had on the early believers and people they met.

Learn and remember verse:
'Call to me, and I will answer you; I will tell you wonderful and marvellous things that you know nothing about.' Jeremiah 33:3

The song 'Call to me', from *Bitesize Bible Songs 2*, puts these words to music and can be downloaded from www.scriptureunion.org.uk/light.

The all-age service outline that is part of this series is 'We're in this together!' on page 117, focusing on Acts 20:13–38 and Exodus 4:18–21.

July – Sept
10

Team work

Bible passage: Acts 18:1–23
Session aim: To acknowledge how God's people work together to share the good news

Theme introduction

Invite someone working full-time to bring God's good news to people to tell a story about someone they work with. Encourage them to keep it short, succinct, child-friendly and free from jargon, preferably with something visual to help people listen and remember. This person could have worked abroad or be working in your local area, either helping with people's physical needs, telling them about Jesus, or a combination of the two. Explain that the early Christians worked together to share God's good news, which is what the children are going to discover in their session.

Song suggestions

'Who was the man?'	*LFE*
'Call to me'	*BSBS2*
'Reach up!'	*RU*
'First and last'	*BSBS*
'Tell out, my soul'	*SOF 520*
'Good news, good news'	*SOF 739*
'We have a gospel to proclaim'	*SOF 1583*

Prayer activity

Split the congregation into small groups and give each group a postcard on which is written:

a) the name of a person or situation that needs another Christian or Christian group to help them
b) the specific help that they need.

For example, a church you know needs help to run a holiday club, someone needs help in their home, or a mission partner has asked for a financial gift.

Someone in each group should pray for this need and, on a set signal, someone should take the postcard to the next group. This can continue for at least three prayer times. Conclude by drawing attention to the fact that you need to work together – not only to pray but also to be the answers to prayer.

Extra idea

Play a game of 'Chinese whispers' with the *Learn and remember* verse, Jeremiah 33:3. Talk about how we only know Jesus because the first believers told people who told people who told people... and so on, until someone told the person who told us!

You could listen to this story from *The Big Bible Storybook* audio book, 'Paul makes new friends'.

Working together

Bible passage: Acts 18:24–28
Session aim: To see how knowing more about Jesus helps his people to share the good news

Theme introduction

Many people will have been away over the summer, so have a time for people to share their news with others. Encourage them to share what they have enjoyed, and also anything good which God did this summer. Make sure you keep each item short.

A fun way to do this is for an adult to stand at the front and light a match when a person starts talking and when they blow it out, the person has to stop! Alternatively, use a stopwatch or similar timer on someone's phone.

In advance, you could ask people to bring photos or souvenirs or create a slide show.

Song suggestions

'There is a voice that must be heard'	SOF 1545
'Jesus, what a beautiful name'	ts 301
'Jesus, Jesus, holy and anointed one'	ts 286
'Call to me'	BSBS2
'All I once held dear'	SOF 646

Extra idea

Priscilla and Aquila are good examples of people who discipled a younger Christian within a home, to help them know Jesus better. As the autumn term begins, it would be appropriate to talk about the various small groups or meetings (for all ages) that will happen in people's homes during the coming week or, more broadly, small groups that will take place anywhere. This might include introducing all the leaders of the children's groups, and the members of each home group.

You could make more of this by commissioning the leaders of all children's and youth groups at the start of the academic year. They could come to the front or stand in small groups, with members of the congregation placing a hand upon their shoulder.

Pray for everyone who will be in a group this week, and take the opportunity to pray for those who lead them.

Prayer activity

Spend time thanking God for the good news from the summer that people have shared. When you have remembered each news item, say the line, 'We thank you, God' and invite the congregation to say, 'for this good news'. To make this more interactive, one side of the congregation could say 'good' and the other 'news'.

Riot in Ephesus

Bible reading: Acts 19:1–12,23–41
Session aim: To explore how people react to the good news in different ways

Theme introduction

Sometimes, the same news can provoke very different reactions within a group of people. Split your congregation in half, labelling one, 'Manchester United' and the other, 'Manchester City', or whatever is appropriate. Read out the following piece of news and ask each group in turn to call out what they would say in response to the news:

Groups: Manchester United and Manchester City fans
News: The top player in Man U is being transferred to City.

Re-name the groups as below, and read the subsequent piece of news.

Groups: Parents and children
News: It's snowing!

Groups: Parents and children
News: It's Christmas next week!

Groups: Pedestrians and cyclists
News: A new pavement cycle track is opening.

Groups: Girls and boys
News: The girls are the winners!

Finish by saying that the good news that Jesus had come so that we can be friends with God was received differently by different people. It still is, and this is what the children are going to find out.

Song suggestions

'Joy to the world'	SOF 314
'The way remix'	BSBS2
'Call to me'	BSBS2
'Come on and celebrate'	SOF 73

Prayer activity

Bring in several newspapers for people to search out some *good news* stories. Point out that news on television, online and in papers is often quite negative, only showing bad things that happen. Then give out some magazines from mission or charity organisations, and ask people to search for and call out some 'good news'. Invite people to say simple one-line prayers thanking God that in a world where things often look bad, he is at work bringing good news to people.

Extra idea

Did you know that the United Nations has declared that every year 21 September should be observed as a day of global ceasefire and non-violence? Peace throughout the world would be great news indeed, but even that would provoke a mixed reaction. Pray for any global trouble spots in the light of this day (Tuesday), especially if there are places where Christians are subjected to violence because of their faith, or war-torn places where the church is under threat.

Listening to the good news

Bible reading: Acts 20:1–16
Session aim: To see how God's people lived their lives as followers of Jesus

Theme introduction

Show a map of Greece and ask if people know which country it is. Talk about the countries that are near Greece and ask for their names including Syria, Lebanon and Turkey. Ask if anyone has been on holiday to any of these places. If possible, contact people in advance and use some of their holiday photos to show what the places look like now. In particular, use photos of things which would have been there years ago, such as hills, olive trees, and the sea. (Some photos are available to download from **web ref AASA3. starters_24–26**.) If you can do a brief interview with an individual or family who have been to Greece, Syria, Lebanon or Turkey, find out where they went and what is was like, especially if they visited any ancient places linked with stories in the Bible. Say that this whole area was where Paul travelled with other followers of Jesus, spreading the good news.

Song suggestions

'I have decided to follow Jesus'	MP 272
'Call to me'	BSBS2
'Bind us together'	SOF 43
'I want to serve the purpose of God'	SOF 260
'In my life, Lord, be glorified'	ts 230

Prayer activity

Read through the items on your news-sheet, commenting on who is meeting who and where, and who is doing what. After each item, invite everyone to pray for those people. You could have a few seconds of silent prayer after each item and then one person could pray out loud or use a simple repeated prayer such as, 'God, please be with them and help them know you more.' Challenge people to do this again at home during the week for the people who are meeting that day.

Extra idea

Learn a song together in another language to remember that God's people are worshipping him together in many places all over the world. It could be something like 'We are marching in the light of God', which has been translated into various languages. The words for this song in another language are on **web ref AASA3. starters_23**.

You could contact a mission partner to see if they have a simple song you could learn, to remember the believers worshipping in the country they live in. You could also search for a song your congregation knows well on YouTube, to find a version sung by people in another language.

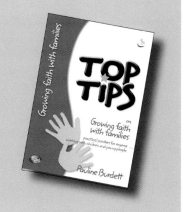

PART TWO

All-age service outlines

These 15 service outlines have followed the tested format of Scripture Union's *Light for the Lectionary* books and earlier material from *Light Years* and *SALT for all ages*. Some of the suggested activities may seem unusual but why not give them a go, or adapt them to fit your situation more precisely? All-age services are usually fairly creative, so one suggestion in this book may stimulate several ideas of your own.

Each service outline contains the following:

Aims: keep these in mind throughout the service to ensure that you remain focused on what you are exploring. Of course, you may wish to rephrase the aims but then, don't lose sight of your own aims. Clear aims help to evaluate a service; so afterwards, try to consider how well you communicated and then how well the children responded. What have you learned from leading this service and what might you do differently as a result?

Getting started: some background information sets the outline and its content in a wider context.

You will need: preparing for all-age services is time-consuming but this checklist should be useful. Necessary downloads are listed but alternatives are usually suggested for those who do not use the Internet. All downloads are available for free on the Scripture Union website: www.scriptureunion.org.uk/light and are listed in service order.

Beginning the service: it is important to start well. These suggestions are varied in style and if one option would not work for you, the suggestion in another service could spark an alternative idea. The Starters in Part One contain plenty of other options. Right from the start, aim to create a sense of community.

Bible reading: almost all outlines include an Old Testament and a New Testament reading, even though only one of these may be the focus of the service. Public reading of the Bible is vitally important and it needs to be done in a way that captures the attention of all present. Creative suggestions are given throughout the 15 outlines. Occasional suggestions have been given for **Bible retelling**.

Bible talk: plenty of interactivity has been built into the Bible talk, recognising that people learn in different ways. The basic framework is given but the speaker will need to adapt to their own style

and circumstances.

Prayer activity: communicating with God can be done in many different ways. The suggestions in the outlines involve activity for individuals, groups and the whole congregation. But do not forget that sometimes we need to meet with God in stillness.

Prayer of confession: church traditions vary in how much emphasis they place specifically on acknowledging our sin and seeking God's forgiveness. This is one option that may fit in with your regular style or it may be something quite different that you could explore further.

Prayer of intercession: outsiders expect Christians to pray for them and the world in need. It is valuable to include people of all ages in leading these prayers.

Ending the service: a good ending is important since it sends people into the coming week with a clear sense of what God has been saying to them and prepared to make a difference for him in his world.

Helpful extras: Music and song ideas are given. The songbooks that are used are listed on page 7 but this list is not exclusive. A **Statement of faith** may not be part of your tradition but it is a useful means of drawing people together in a resolve to know and serve God. **Games** are suggested, some of which are available as free downloads. These are especially important for providing for young children and anyone whose preferred learning style is of a more active nature.

Notes and comments: extra ideas and explanation may help you in your preparation. Extra ideas, of course, are also available in Part One, in the starter suggestions, linked to the *Light* theme you are exploring.

Downloads: these are to be found for free on the Scripture Union website www.scriptureunion.org.uk/light. A download is referenced according to the volume (**AASA3.**), the month, if you were using it in the *Light* cycle (**Oct**), and then consecutive numbers (**_2**) – for example, **web ref AASA3.Oct_2**. The downloads include word documents providing necessary templates or scripts as well as PowerPoint presentations or video clips.

If you are going to use a DVD clip, check its certification and, if necessary, obtain permission from the parents of young children for them to see the clip. You should also ensure that your church holds the relevant licence to show film clips; details of the Church Video Licence are available at www.ccli.co.uk. You may also want to use worship CDs/DVDs, such as Hillsongs Kids CD/DVDs *Superhero, Superstrong God* and *Great Big God*.

Please note that it is your responsibility to check the veracity of any information downloaded from the Internet and to check the conditions for playing or displaying any audio or digital material and its copyright status. You cannot assume that any images on any site listed in this book can automatically be copied and shared with your congregation by any means without checking for further details and gaining permission where necessary. We have sought wherever possible to ensure that our suggestions fall within copyright law and Scripture Union does not accept responsibility for any copyright infringements by individuals using this book to prepare material for

Golden rules for all-age worship

The foundational key for leading effective all-age worship is thinking about it as a family time (the church family), not as a time for the children with the adults present, or as an adult worship time with the children present. It's an all-age time – a totally unique 'brand' of worship.

This three-point checklist will help you in your planning worship when all ages are present.

1. Is it appropriate?
Is what I am planning – simple and uncomplicated? It should be!
Is what I am planning – childish or embarrassing or patronising? It should NOT be.

Example: language is one thing to be really aware of. It needs to be simple and clear, although the concept may be understood on several levels.
NOT: Let's come before the Lord in penitence for our transgressions.
NOT: Now we're going to say sorry for the naughty things we've done.
BUT: We're going to spend some time saying sorry to God for the things we've done wrong. (Simple, uncomplicated language that connects with everyone.)

2. Is it moving at the right pace?
Variety is crucial, (fast-moving and busy, reflective and still) and it is not necessarily older people who like stillness and vice versa!
As a general rule, aim for one activity to last no longer than 7 minutes.

3. How much interaction is there?
Option 1: interaction between the leader and congregation
Option 2: interaction amongst the congregation
Option 3: interaction between the congregation and God

Interaction should never be forced upon anyone and should never be forced or artificial for the sake of 'doing something'. Never separate an activity into say 'a song for the children' for that will alienate adults. Instead, for example, say, 'We'll sing another song now.'

Examples: movement; singing and making music (and repetition helps the youngest to the oldest join in); stories; puppets; sign language; using all the senses; mime; construction/craft; engaging with symbols and artefacts; humour and emotion.

As a service leader
• Remember that you are leading people together into God's presence
• Be enthusiastic and enjoy yourself
• Prepare well and work with others
• Never be apologetic for what you are leading

This has been adapted from Golden rules for all-worship by Jo Squires
© 2008 BIG Ministries www.bigministries.co.uk and used with permission.

Spectators at the cross

October

Light series: Jesus our Saviour
Light readings: The passion narratives from all four Gospels

Aims: to meet the people who watched Jesus die
to explore our different responses to Jesus' death

Readings: Psalm 22:1–8,14–18; Mark 15:24–30,33–47

Getting started

In October 2009, *Light* explores the death and resurrection (using all four Gospel accounts) in a way that is not possible at Easter-time, when the whole story is often crammed into two Sundays, getting to the resurrection far too quickly. It is not helpful either that, inevitably, the Easter story comes at the end of a school term when children and group leaders are often tired and less receptive. So this series gives children's workers the opportunity to reflect in detail not only on the events but also on the meaning of the cross. This service, using Mark's Gospel as a focus, complements the *Light* series. It can be used at any point during the month, and could be easily adapted for use at any time in the year, especially Good Friday.

Several groups of people gathered around the foot of the cross – the regular spectators at such events, the Roman soldiers with a job to do and those who loved Jesus. Jesus' death is deeply moving and you would want to provoke a suitable age-appropriate response from everyone. You would not want young children to be upset by the goriness of the story but at the same time, you do not want to make it all so emotionally toothless that the power of the cross to evoke a response is lost! Jesus' death is at the heart of what makes us Christians.

You will need:

- four actors and props for the **Beginning the service** sketch and props for a radio reporter
- download: **web ref AASA3.Oct_1** – Psalm 22 for **Bible reading**
- **web ref AASA3.Oct_2** – three pairs of spectacle frames for **Bible talk** and **Prayers of confession**
- **web ref AASA3.Oct_3** – **Statement of faith**

Beginning the service

With: four actors, dressed appropriately for their part (this will need rehearsing); mobile phone; a bus stop sign; a microphone and props for a radio reporter

Three actors stand patiently at the bus stop – an old lady, the grandchild/relative of this lady, someone wearing a uniform for work (eg a businessman, shop assistant, air hostess). The old lady collapses and the relative anxiously tries to help while the person in uniform rings for an ambulance on their mobile. Almost immediately the fourth actor arrives (a paramedic or a passing nurse/doctor, suitably dressed). They resuscitate the old lady, who is led away by her relative.

Holding a microphone, you ask the relative, uniformed person and paramedic/nurse/doctor to come forward to be interviewed. You are a radio reporter and you want to find out exactly what happened. Each gives a brief account of how the incident affected them. You want to demonstrate that the person's response depended upon their relationship to the woman.

- The uniformed person just happened to be on their way to work and did what they could, but were emotionally detached. They have almost forgotten about it because it was not significant to them.
- The relative was deeply affected because this was someone they love and they thought she was dying. They are so relieved she is OK.
- The paramedic was just doing their job. They are sad that it happened, but they are always encountering situations like this. They are glad it turned out OK.

Introduce the theme of the service: you are going to look at the different responses of the spectators who watched Jesus die. Put the theme into the context of the *Light* programme as appropriate.

Bible reading

Psalm 22:1–8,14–18
Mark 15:24–30,33–47

Background sad music could be played for both readings. For example, Samuel Barber's *Adagio for strings*.

The reading from Mark 15:24–30,33–47 can be read with a narrator and several people taking the parts of Jesus and the onlookers.

Introduce Psalm 22:1–8,14–18 by saying that, although written hundreds of years before Jesus died, it describes what happened to him. Jesus, hanging on the cross, even quoted from this psalm. Ask people to listen with their eyes closed to imagine the desperation of the writer. Two readers, standing apart, should read the verses about the pain, while the facts about God in verses 3–5 should be read by a third reader.

The version of this reading from the CEV, is available as a download from **web ref AASA3. Oct_1**. 'Voice 1' stands to the left; 'Voice 2' is centred; 'Voice 3' is to the right.

Bible talk

With: three sets of large cardboard frames of a pair of spectacles, with the following images duplicated in both 'lens': the outline of three crosses in a line, all exactly the same, with a body hanging on each; a coat lying on the ground with some coins beside it; a wooden plaque above a cross with these words carved into it – This is the King of the Jews. These are available as a PowerPoint download from **web ref AASA3. Oct_2**.

Remind people of the different responses to the collapse of the old lady. It all depended upon who they were and their relationship to her. You are now going to look at the response of three groups of spectators to Jesus' death on the cross. At this point, you will want to be sure that everyone has some idea about Jesus' death. Do not assume that people know much. The *Light* theme has focused on the story of the cross, so there is scope to recap what the children and young people have discovered, linking the all-age service and Sunday groups. Check how far into the series they are by the time of this service. Suggest people keep their Bibles open at Mark 15 (if available) since you are going to briefly go through the story. Try to use 'seeing' and 'spectating' words as you comment on the story.

Regular spectators
Show the first glasses frame. If you have real frames, put these on the nose of a volunteer. The first group of spectators watching Jesus were the regular people who turned up at any public event or spectacle – a fight, a wedding, the visit of a celebrity. They had no commitment to Jesus even though they had probably come across him before as he had preached in the temple and ridden into Jerusalem on a donkey. They had come to **see** a celebrity death (vs 29,30,35–36)! Make the connection with the person in uniform who watched the old lady collapse at the bus stop. Comment on how the spectators mocked Jesus, gave him wine to drink (to numb the pain – although Luke says this was the soldiers, Luke

23:36,37) and heard him crying out to God. They misinterpreted what Jesus said, thinking he was crying out for the prophet Elijah (which sounds like 'Eloi', the word for 'God'). **These people just saw Jesus as an interesting person who had nothing to do with them. They were emotionally detached.**

Soldiers doing their job

Show the second glasses frame. (Or, if you have real frames, ask a second volunteer to wear them.) The soldiers were just doing their job (vs 24–28). They regularly put people to death. Jesus was just another one of at least three that day! Make the connection with the paramedic. They may not even have **looked** at Jesus with any interest, but were interested in his coat, **seeing** it as an opportunity to benefit by gambling over who should own it. John says that it was a coat made without a seam, so it could not be divided between them (John 19:23,24). **These were people who hardly noticed who Jesus was.** But comment on the fact that the army officer **noticed** that Jesus was different, whatever he meant by saying Jesus was the Son of God.

Jesus' family and friends

Show the third glasses frame (or ask for a third volunteer to wear them, if you have them). Jesus' family and friends were **watching** from far off. For them, his death was awful (vs 40–47). Make the connection with the relative of the old lady at the bus stop. This was the man they really loved and who they hoped would change everything. They **saw** him as the 'King of the Jews', the title that Pilate had ordered to be written above Jesus' head, but Jesus was much more than that to them. Talk about John's account of the provision that Jesus made for his mother (John 19:26,27). They must have heard about the strange tearing of the curtain in the temple. (Explain the significance of this, as a sign that access to God was no longer limited just to the very few people who occasionally could go behind the curtain to meet with God.) They did what they could and gave him a decent burial, although there was not time to do everything they would have liked. **Jesus' death deeply mattered to these people, even though they did not understand.**

People respond in different ways to Jesus' death, even today.
- Some people are not bothered about his death and see it as just an old story.
- Some people may have heard about Jesus a bit but are so busy with their everyday lives that they don't think too much about him.
- Some people are intrigued by Jesus and have come to love him and admire him. It was only after the resurrection that Jesus' friends began

to understand. The more that people hear about Jesus and love him, the more they will grow in their understanding of what his death and resurrection mean.

Jesus felt utterly alone as he hung on the cross. Even God his father had turned away from him. Jesus had taken all the wrong in the world onto his own shoulders and God could not bear to look at him. Quote some verses from Psalm 22 to make sure people see his desolation. Only after he came alive again did it become obvious that Jesus' death was not a mistake. Notice that he shouted out loud as a sign that he was not defeated, and then he died. John says he shouted, 'Everything is done/finished!' (John 19:30) The wrong of the world could not finish him off; he was alive. He had defeated all that is evil.

Imagine you are putting on your glasses to look at Jesus as he died on the cross. Will you see him as someone interesting but nothing more? Will you see him as someone who might have something important to say but you are too busy to think much about it? Or will you want to know more and love him because he died?

It would be appropriate to sing 'When I think about the cross' or a similar song followed by the **Prayers of confession.**

Prayers of confession

With: a symbol of, or a real, empty cross

Ask everyone to look at the cross and then close their eyes to imagine Jesus on it. You could give younger children a picture of the cross to hold. First imagine you are like the crowds, standing around the cross and talking about what is going on. After a few moments, pray along the following lines:

Father God, we are sorry that sometimes we hear about the story of Jesus' death and we don't think it matters to us at all. We are not bothered.

Imagine you are like the soldiers, getting on with their job and too busy to notice anything. After a few moments, pray:

Father God, we are sorry that sometimes we are so busy that we don't have time to think about how much you love us and how much Jesus has done for us on the cross.

Imagine you are like Jesus' friends and family. After a few moments, pray:
Father God, help us to understand and take Jesus' death on the cross more seriously. Jesus died for

the wrong things we have done. Please forgive us for all the wrong we have done this week. Help us to make a new start this day! (Pause)

God promised that he will forgive all those who ask for forgiveness!

Prayers of intercession

With: a PowerPoint, acetate or individual prayer point sheets, which are written inside the lens of a pair of spectacles

All through his life, Jesus saw a world in need. Prepare prayer points that focus on places of need where there is wrong that needs to be righted and also on areas where, as a church, you are helping people to see Jesus as he really is. Either all together or in small groups, pray together, remembering that this is the world that Jesus died for. You could create a PowerPoint presentation with visual images of prayer points inside the frames of a pair of glasses; see **web ref AASA3.Oct_2.**

Ending the service

With: two long, used matchsticks for everyone (or similar); wool

Everyone should bind together the two sticks into a cross shape, to take home as a reminder of the service. Talk about where at home you might put it. You could conclude with the **Statement of faith** and/or with a triumphant song to emphasise that Jesus' death was not in vain and is vitally important today!

Helpful extras

Music and song ideas
'When I think about the cross' (ks 376); 'Led like a lamb to the slaughter' (ts 312); 'When I survey the wondrous cross' (ts 572) there are several new tunes and Stuart Townend's 'Oh to see the dawn' (SOF 2020). Scripture Union's *Bitesize Bible Songs* and *Bitesize Bible Songs 2* contain Bible verses in song which are ideal to use with children in an all-age context, especially the song 'So much' on *Bitesize Bible Songs 2 CD*. For more details visit www.scriptureunion.org.uk/light.

Notes and comments

Top Tips on Explaining the Cross to Children and Young People (SU) is a key book to use in ensuring that you clearly explain the meaning of the cross to an all-age audience – see page 87.

To tell the story of the cross, you could show an episode of the story of the cross from one of Scripture Union's holiday club programmes. Alternatively, read the retold Bible story of Jesus' death and resurrection from *The 10 Must Know Stories* by Heather Butler or *Must Know Stories* by Robert Harrison, both published by Scripture Union. Details of these are on page 70.

A celebration of Holy Communion can very naturally be incorporated into this service.

If your church has a cross in a prominent position, use it during the service as a visual point for prayer or response.

You should be expecting people of all ages to make some sort of response to God. Be prepared with suitable literature, such as *Jesus=Friendship forever, Me + Jesus, Friends with Jesus,* for children and young people, along with what you usually have for adult enquirers. The new book *Top Tips on Helping a Child Respond to Jesus* would also be valuable. For more details, visit www. scriptureunion.org.uk.

There is plenty of scope for personal testimony about what Jesus' death has meant to a member of the church community. This needs to be in clear, non-jargon, inclusive language.

This service outline is appropriate to use for an all-age service over the Easter period. In *The All-Age Service Annual Volume Three* there is not a service outline for Good Friday or Easter Day, although an outline for both services is available on www.scriptureunion.org.uk/light in the *Light for the Lectionary* section, **web ref 2.4.10_1** for Good Friday and **web ref 4.4.10_1** for Easter Day.

Trusting God in the tough times

November

Light series: Birth of a nation
Light readings: Exodus 2:1–25; 3:1 – 4:20; 11:1 – 12:30; 14:1–31

Aims: to see how hard it was for Moses to lead God's people
to see just how much God can be trusted

Readings: Exodus 5:1 – 6:13; 2 Corinthians 11:21b–31; 12:8–10

Getting started

The *Light* series for this month centres on the early part of Moses' story. Moses was called by God to do a job for which he felt totally underqualified – to lead the Israelites out of slavery in Egypt to the Promised Land. Not only was Moses bad at public speaking, but when he and Aaron obeyed God, Pharaoh made life worse for the Israelites. They, in turn, blamed Moses. Moses had a tough job on his hands!

In this service, we will explore what it means to trust in God when life is tough. How much dare we trust God to be right, to do what is right and to command what is right? The example of Paul, who faithfully spread the gospel despite dozens of difficulties and potential obstacles, encourages perseverance. This topic should be very relevant to many, and not just to the people who are known to be having a tough time. Aim to get the balance in offering hope and the reassurance of God's care, whilst also allowing people to be honest.

Make space for prayer support and outline the facilities your church provides for people in need. Encourage the congregation to act in practical ways, being there for each other outside of the church service.

You will need:

- a hand-held microphone for **Beginning the service**
- copies of Exodus 5:1 – 6:13 for the **Bible reading**
- a roll of paper with graffiti writing for the **Bible talk** – statements are also available from **web ref AASA3.Nov_1**
- the means to learn 2 Corinthians 12:9 (as a visual or audio version)

Beginning the service

With: a hand-held microphone (if possible)

Ask the congregation to chat to the people sitting around them. They are to briefly describe (in just a couple of sentences each) their best and worst moments this week. Begin by briefly talking about your best and worst moment.

Try to keep your 'worst moment' as light-hearted as possible. Not everyone will feel comfortable speaking so personally – this gives them the option of joining in without feeling awkward, whilst getting them to think about tough situations they are experiencing. The idea of this activity is simply to introduce people to the theme of the service.

Ask for volunteers of different ages to briefly share. Take the hand-held mike to them or ask them to shout out their answers. Keep this as informal as possible.

Bible reading

Use a modern version of Exodus 5:1 – 6:13 such as *The Message*. Mark up a copy for five volunteers - a narrator, Moses (and Aaron), Pharaoh and God.

2 Corinthians 11:21b–31; 12:8–10 is a dramatic declaration, so ensure that the reader has practised to enable them to read it with feeling. If the volunteer could learn it by heart, so much the better. The words of God in 2 Corinthians 12:9 could be read by another reader or be announced through the PA system.

Bible talk

With: one or two volunteers willing to speak about trusting God in tough times; a means to learn 2 Corinthians 12:9 – either put the words on display or use the song version, 'My grace' from *Bitesize Bible Songs 2* (SU)

1. Story of suffering

Remind the congregation of the examples of 'worst moments' from **Beginning the service**. Choose examples of 'worst moments' which reflect examples relevant to a wide age range.

Alternatively, display the following examples of situations and feelings that members of your congregation might have experienced. They could be put up on a roll of paper, as a graffiti wall. These statements, in different fonts, are also available as a download from **web ref AASA3.Nov_1**.

In the lives of children:
I fell over in the playground.
My best friend and I fell out at school!
The cat got sick.

In the lives of teenagers:
I broke up with my boyfriend.
I overheard her gossiping about me.
I don't know what I am going to do next!

Parents:
I just can't find time for everything!
I am exhausted!
We always seem to be arguing these days.

Older people:
I'm so lonely.
The doctor told me I had got to start the treatment next Wednesday.
I don't know how we are going to pay the bills.

General:
I feel so underappreciated at work.
I lost my job this week.
I've got nothing to look forward to.

Briefly talk about the difficult situation the Israelites were experiencing in slavery as Pharaoh made their lives even more impossible. How would they have felt about God and their identity? Talk about how difficult it must have been to trust in God and have hope for the future. Put this in the context of what the children have done so far in their *Light* groups.

2. Finding God in tough times

Ask someone (prepare them before the service) to share their experience of going to God and finding him to be there in the middle of a tough time. Ask them to be honest and real about their doubts, their struggles and what comfort God brought them. It would be better to do this as an interview because that helps to keep to time and also to probe if the speaker is not illustrating the point as much as is necessary.

Remind the congregation of what Moses said to God in Exodus 5:22,23 after Pharaoh refused to let the Israelites go and, instead, commanded that bricks were made without the straw being provided. Point out that Moses was real with God – 'you haven't done a thing to help.' He asked honest questions in order to seek God's will in the situation. Then comment on what God said in reply in Exodus 6:1–8. Talk about how Moses found confidence and reassurance as he conversed with God.

3. Persevering when everything seems to remain tough

Ask someone (perhaps the same person) to speak about continuing to trust in God when a difficult situation doesn't seem to change over a long period of time. What advice would they give to someone in a similar situation?

Point out how difficult it must have been for Moses to continue to trust in God when Pharaoh didn't listen and things apparently got worse rather than better. Even God's own people, the Israelites, didn't believe him!

Refer to Paul's huge list of relentlessly tough situations and talk about his ability to persevere despite difficulties. Ask if anyone can remember what God said to Paul in 2 Corinthians 12:9.

At this point, display this verse so that it can be explored as a *Learn and remember* verse. One side of the congregation should repeat half of what God said, while the other side speaks the rest. Then swap sides. Alternatively, use the song 'My grace', a song version of the verse, from *Bitesize Bible Songs 2*: see **Music and song ideas**.

4. Keeping the bigger picture in sight

Paul suffered for the sake of the gospel. He accepted his sufferings because he saw the goal and purpose in his life. In every situation, he knew God would use it for good. He was able to identify with Christ's sufferings. He lived by God's strength and for his glory. Paul kept the end goal in sight – God's victory and God's glory.

Encourage everyone to seek God's peace and purpose in their own tough personal situations. Pray that everyone will know God with them in any challenges they face this week.

Prayer activity

Remind everyone that the people of Israel were very burdened by their slavery. Paul himself suffered in many ways. But God was with his people to rescue. them But even more important, he was *with them* in their time of trouble.

Often we talk about someone who is troubled as someone who is 'bowed down'. Ask everyone to get into circles of about twelve people. Each person should turn to face the person on their right, check that they know their name, and then stoop their shoulders and place a hand on their neighbour's shoulder. They should then pray for this person by name, even though they may not know the details of whatever is troubling them.

After a few moments, invite everyone to stand up straight and raise their chins. Then read Leviticus

26:13. This is what God said to the people of Israel after they had left Egypt. God calls us to walk tall. Pray for everyone present that this week they may know God with them, giving them hope.

Make sure that there are opportunities for people with particular needs to be prayed with by others in the congregation.

Ending the service

With: paper cut to the size of bookmarks (enough for one each); pens

Explain that on one side of the bookmark they should write the name of (or draw) one person they will pray for this week who they know is having a tough time. On the other side of the bookmark, they should write 'God's power is strongest when we are weak.'

Remind the congregation of God's faithfulness and his ever-willingness to listen. Conclude with a collective prayer of thanks that God is with us and encourage everyone to always keep the bigger picture in mind. Finish by singing 'When I survey the wondrous cross' or a song that recalls how God knows all about suffering because, in Christ, he too suffered.

Helpful extras

Music and song ideas
'When I survey the wondrous cross' (ks 376); 'Even though I walk (You never let go)' by Matt Redman (SOF 1753); 'Faithful One' (SOF 89); 'Blessed be your name' by Matt and Beth Redman (SOF 1193)

'My grace' is a *Learn and remember* verse on *Bitesize Bible Songs 2* (SU) or it can be bought as a single item download – see www.scriptureunion.org.uk/light.

Notes and comments

Pray that you will get the right balance between offering hope to those who are struggling and being genuinely supportive. Make sure that services for those going through a difficult time are well-advertised – prayer support, practical support, meals, visits, pastoral support groups. Pray specifically for these ministries in a time of intercession.

Don't forget any mission partners who may be going through tough times. If your church has the facilities, set up a video link with them for a live interview. Alternatively, ask them to write a short update paragraph.

Scripture Union resources for Christmas

Three Christmas resource books that contain practically everything you need for Christmas time – Advent suggestions, nativity plays, family events and carol services. *The Big Red Book* is full of Christmas ideas to use with under fives.

More Christmas Wrapped Up!
978 1 84427 261 7
£9.99

Christmas Wrapped Up!
978 1 85999 795 6
£9.99

The Big Red Book
978 1 85999 658 4
£9.99

These multi-sensory resource books are suitable for church services, but also for youth groups, small groups and individuals They include the use of visual images downloadable from the Internet, music and lots of creative interactivity. Suitable to use in Advent but appropriate for any time of the year.

Mary – A Journey of Discovery
978 1 84427 184 9
£9.99

Angels – a Journey of Exploration
978 1 84427 223 0
£9.99

Great Christmas gifts to give to young children in an all-age service or in a toddler group

Happy Christmas
978 1 84277 284 6
75p

My Little Red Book (Tiddlywinks)
978 1 85999 659 1
£3.50

Gifts for a King
978 1 84427 179 5
99p

Jesus is born (Little fish)
978 0 85421 963 6
75p

The Long Journey
978 1 84427 177 1
99p

The Shepherds' Surprise
978 1 84427 178 8
99p

Journey to Bethlehem Advent Calendar
978 1 84427 354 6
£3.99

A Message for Mary
978 1 84427 176 4
99p

Bible resources

These are all Scripture Union story books that you can use to bring Bible stories alive in an all-age service. *The Big Bible Storybook* is especially suitable for under fives and is available as a book and an audio book. Suggestions are made in Part 1 for specific stories that link with the theme of a session.

The Big Bible Storybook
(hardback)
978 1 84427 228 0
£12.99

The Strong Tower
978 1 84427 122 1
£7.99

10 Must Know Stories
978 1 84427 326 3
£3.99

Must Know Stories
978 1 84427 320 1
£7.99

The Big Bible Storybook
(audio book)
978 1 84427 379 9
£19.99

Make sure that everyone knows what Bible reading guides are available, to equip people to meet with God regularly as they read the Bible. Make a special effort to encourage families to read the Bible together. This is the time for New Year resolutions!

Encourage people to visit www.wordlive.org, Scripture Union's online Bible reading site.

Prices are correct at the time of going to print. All are available from good Christian bookshops or Scripture Union Mail Order or online – www.scriptureunion.org.uk/shop

Mary waits and waits

Advent/December

Light series: Christmas Praise!
Light readings: Luke 1,2

Aims: to see how Mary, as a Jew, waited for the Messiah, and then waited
for Jesus' birth
to recognise that in Advent we also wait for Jesus' return

Readings: Isaiah 9:6,7; Luke 1:26–45

Getting started

Not surprisingly, this Advent service, as part of the *Light* Christmas Praise! series, looks at the early part
of the nativity story. The secular world uses the term 'Advent' to mark the beginning of the final run
up to Christmas. This is characterised by Advent calendars and candles which begin on 1 December,
whatever the date the Church recognises as Advent Sunday. There is no real distinction between Advent
and Christmas, between waiting and celebrating. Christians, on the other hand, recognise the value of
discovering God in the waiting, an essential part of this annual celebration. Mary waited and waited, for
a long nine months and, in effect, much longer since as a Jewish woman she had been waiting for the
coming of the Messiah all her life. Elizabeth, her cousin, was also caught up in this waiting.

The material for this service uses the visual theme of a wrapped present to connect with the worldly
preoccupation with gifts and shopping at this time of the year. Research shows that people on the fringe
of the Church are more willing to attend worship in December than at any other time of year. This
provides a great opportunity to welcome people of all ages, but particularly families, to a well-planned,
informal time of worship where they will feel comfortable. May you be able to provide this for your
congregation.

You will need:

- a beautifully wrapped present
- a version of Isaiah 9:6, available as a download
  web ref AASA3.Dec_1 for **Beginning the service**
- cards with the 11 missing names from the Gospel
  reading or a version of Luke 1:26–45 downloaded
  from **web ref AASA3.Dec_2** for the **Bible reading**
- strips of paper and pens to use for the game of
  'Consequences' for the **Bible talk**
- two completed Bible story consequences which
  can be downloaded from **web ref AASA3.Dec_3** for
  the **Bible talk**
- materials for the four prayer areas in the **Prayer activity**

Beginning the service

With: a beautifully wrapped present; on display, a copy of Isaiah 9:6 – the CEV version below is also available as a download from **web ref AASA3. Dec_1**

Display your wrapped present. (An image of it could be projected onto a screen instead.) Point to the present and ask who gets excited about opening Christmas presents. Remind everyone that it is not yet time to open presents. There is still a lot of waiting to be done until Christmas Day. There is a lot about waiting in today's service, but reassure everyone that there is not too much waiting or hanging about involved!

Explain that many Christians use the season of Advent, the four weeks leading up to Christmas, to prepare to celebrate the birth of Jesus and to remember that they are also waiting for the day when Jesus will return to earth as a glorious King.

Learn Isaiah 9:6, part of the Old Testament passage for this service, as an extended *Learn and remember* verse. This verse explains that Jesus came as a baby, but would also be a mature and holy ruler. The leader could read the italicised type; the women and girls could proclaim the section in regular type, the men and boys could reply with the words in bold type. Practise saying it several times.

A child has been born for us.
We have been given a son.
Who will be our ruler.
His names will be
Wonderful Adviser and Mighty God,
Eternal Father and Prince of Peace.
Isaiah 9:6

Bible reading
Luke 1:26–45

With: cards displaying the following names: Gabriel, Nazareth, Galilee, Joseph, David, Mary, Jesus, Elizabeth, Israel, Judea, Zechariah; a version of the reading in Word, and also a digital version with the names missing, to be completed by the click of a mouse. They are all available as a download from **web ref AASA3.Dec_2**

The reading from Luke 1:26–46 has come with all the names missing. Explain that everyone will need to help fill in the gaps. Provide all the names on sheets of card. Either ask 11 helpers to come to the front to hold up the cards when asked or, if appropriate, challenge several active children to run to the front to find the correct card and hold

it up once someone has given the right answer. Alternatively, project the reading showing the gaps for the missing words, with the blanks filled in once the answer has been identified.

Read the passage, pausing whenever a name needs to be supplied. Some names will come quickly, others may need a clue or two.

Bible talk

With: a strip of paper and pens for each person to complete a short game of 'Consequences'; two completed strips for demonstration purposes, one for the angel Gabriel and one for Mary, as hard copy on an acetate or flip chart, a version of which can be downloaded from **web ref AASA3.Dec_3**

Have you ever played the game 'Consequences', or 'What happened next?' Explain that everybody has a long strip of paper, which is passed around a group. Everyone fills in a category and then passes it on to the next person so that at the end, there is a basic storyline. In this service, you are going to play a simplified version. Give out a strip of paper and a pen to every person or small group of people. (The leader could complete a sample one to show how it is done.)

Everyone should write down someone's name – suggest the name of a child in the church. (Some people might prefer to draw pictures instead of writing.) Fold the paper over (but unless you can organise this, do not pass them around).

Add another person's name and fold the paper over.

Add the next category – where they met.

The final category is, 'The consequence was…'

At the end, when everyone has filled in their strip, collect in a few to read out. Explain that it takes quite a long time to play the game, so if you were to read out everyone's piece of paper you would be waiting a long time to find out what the 'consequence' would be.

The **Bible reading** was about a whole string of consequences: one thing happened which led to something else. Use the digital consequences or create your own hard copy on a flip chart or acetate.

- It starts with God sending whom? (The first fold displays 'Angel Gabriel'.)
- Where did God send Gabriel? (Unfold 'was sent to Nazareth'.)

- Whom did the angel find in Nazareth? (Unfold 'where he found Mary'.)
- What was Mary doing? (Unfold 'who was waiting'.)

Show the whole sentence.

The consequence of the angel going to Nazareth was that he met Mary. She was a Jewish girl and she had been waiting for a very special day when the Messiah, a very special king, would come from God to help all Jewish people. Mary would have known the same *Learn and remember* verse that we learned earlier. Say the verse again.

A child has been born for us.
We have been given a son.
Who will be our ruler.
His names will be:
Wonderful Adviser and Mighty God,
Eternal Father and Prince of Peace
Isaiah 9:6

Mary was waiting for the Prince of Peace to be born. But what was the consequence of Mary waiting? She was told by the angel that she would have a baby.

Turn to the second consequence strip.

- After the angel had left her, where did Mary go? (Unfold 'Mary went to the hill country'.)
- Whom did Mary visit? (Unfold 'to see Elizabeth'.) Check that everyone knows who Elizabeth is.
- When Mary and Elizabeth got together, there were two amazing consequences. First, what happened to the baby Elizabeth was expecting? (Unfold 'Elizabeth's baby jumped for joy.')
- Then what did Mary and Elizabeth do? (Unfold 'They praised God.')

Show the whole storyline.

Say the *Learn and remember* verse again to see if you too can praise God as a consequence of knowing that God not only came to Mary more than two thousand years ago, but he has come to us and will come again. That is the true meaning of Advent.

If you have not already done this, light the relevant number of candles on the Advent ring.

Prayer activity

Set up four prayer areas, one based on each letter of W-A-I-T. Invite everyone to visit as many of the prayer areas as they choose. Indicate how much time will be available for the activity. If possible, quietly play a Taizé chant, or similar, as background music.

In the **W**ait area, provide a lit candle or a beautifully wrapped present. Psalm 33:20 should be displayed on a card: 'We wait in hope for the Lord; he is our help and our shield' (NIV). Someone could read out the verse and invite everyone to sit silently to wait for God to speak in the quiet.

In the **A**doration, or praise, area, invite everyone to think of one word to describe God. These words can then be written up onto a large sheet of paper. Help children to decide on their chosen word, and then to record it on the paper. Some of the titles for Jesus from Isaiah 9:6 would be appropriate. Display Psalm 34:3 on a card: 'Glorify the Lord with me: let us exalt his name together' (NIV).'

For the **I**ntercessions area, supply sheets of paper and pencils for people to write or draw their prayer requests. Provide a small basket for the completed prayers so they can be gathered together and offered to God. On a card, display Jeremiah 33:3: 'Call to me and I will answer you' (NIV).

To enable everyone to say **T**hanks to God, display on a card, 'Give thanks to the Lord, for he is good; his love endures for ever' (Psalm 118:1) (NIV). Provide a parcel wrapped in plain paper, and sheets of shiny stars or stickers that say 'Thank you'. Invite everyone to think of one particular thing for which they want to thank God, and then place a sticker on the parcel as a way of thanking God.

At the end of this time, as everyone returns to their seats, bring the **A**doration praise sheet, the basket of **I**ntercessory prayers and the **T**hanks prayer parcel covered in stickers to the front. Explain that all these prayers, as well as the silent prayers from the **W**aiting area, will now be offered to God as everyone says the Lord's Prayer together.

Prayers of intercession

Show the consequences from the **Bible talk** and highlight the following points as a way in to prayer.

Angel Gabriel: Pray for everyone who brings God's message to others, which could be anyone who shares the good news of Jesus.

Nazareth: Pray for all who live in Nazareth today, where life is especially difficult. Pray particularly for the few remaining Christians there, who wait for God to come to rescue them.

Mary: Pray for all people who, like Mary, wait on the Lord to hear him speak into their lives.

Waiting: Pray for everyone waiting for news in the run up to Christmas – news of family members and friends, the results of medical tests, of examinations, or of possible redundancy.

Baby: Pray for everyone who is excited as they wait for Christmas that they may know true joy, and not disappointment.

They praised God: Pray that everyone in church will be able to praise God this Advent-time.

Ending the service

Remind everyone that there are always consequences when God sets something in motion. Mary had been waiting for the Messiah to come, and then she found herself waiting for a special baby to be born. The consequence of today's story was that Elizabeth praised God, after she too had been waiting a long time. Will we be praising God on Christmas Day after so much waiting? We have to wait for Christmas, and we have to wait for Jesus to return as the Prince of Peace and our King.

Helpful extras

Music and song ideas
'Soon and very soon' is an easy song for even non-readers to join in (*ts* 460) and includes praise in response to seeing the King; occasional visitors to church may not be clear of the distinction between Advent and Christmas, so they may feel more comfortable if at least one traditional carol is included. A suitable carol would be 'O little town of Bethlehem' (*SOF* 420); an appropriate Taizé song to play during the **Prayer activity** would be 'Wait for the Lord' (*SOF* 1575). *Carol Praise*, published by HarperCollins*Publishers*, contains many new carols and fresh arrangements of older carols. It includes Graham Kendrick's song on Mary's response to the angel, 'Let it be to me'.

The *Learn and remember* song 'God has a plan' based on 1 John 4:9 from the *Bitesize Bible Songs* CD is appropriate to use with this service, acknowledging that God sent his son into this world. It can be purchased as a download from www.scriptureunion.org.uk/light.

Game

'Pass the Parcel' is a game based on waiting for a turn, as well as linking with this service's visual theme of presents. The layers of the game could contain the different names needed to complete the **Bible reading** (in which case ensure the game is played before it), or with the different 'Consequences' answers used in the **Bible talk**.

Notes and comments

The 'Pass the Parcel' game could be played as a gathering activity for children in the few minutes before the service starts.

A hymn or song of praise would be suitable to follow on from the **Bible talk** to encourage people to respond with praise before moving into a time of prayer.

Stars or stickers that say 'Thank you' for use in the **Prayer activity** can be obtained from stationery or birthday shops.

If you have any Advent traditions, such as lighting an Advent candle or opening an Advent calendar, do incorporate that into the service.

To develop the **Prayers of intercession** and the theme of waiting for God to set things in motion, you could encourage anyone who is waiting for something specific to share their experiences.

It may be overdoing the 'Consequences' game idea, but one alternative **Prayer activity** would be to ask everyone to write on a strip of paper the following phrases. After each phrase, they pass the strip around a group, so that everyone ends up with a prayer composed by several people. The phrases are: a name that addresses God; something that God has done that you are thankful for; a promise of God; a request for him to set something in motion; a final request for patience as we wait.

It's the nativity!

Nativity service

Light readings: Luke 1,2

Aim: to remind people of God coming down to earth to rescue his people
to explore the real meaning of Christmas

Readings: Luke 1:26–38; Luke 2:1–20; John 1:1–18 or Isaiah 9:2–7

Getting started

This service outline can be used at any time over the Christmas period. The primary aim of the service
is to help people think about what Christmas really means as the story is heard in its entirety. There are
likely to be visitors in church over Christmas, so make them feel welcome and included.

The Christmas story is familiar to most church people, so it is always challenging to present it in a way
that still feels fresh; but visitors and certainly many children will be hearing it properly for the first time.
Keep these people in mind when you are speaking, rather than assuming prior knowledge. This will help
you to keep your language clear and accessible. It is important too that in your preparation you have
read the story several times over so that you do not add in details that do not come from the story in
the Bible. Reindeers, snowmen and camels are very traditional but do not appear in the real story and
can reduce its power.

You will need:

- vox pop for **Beginning the service** – download from
  web ref AASA3.Nat_1
- a selection of Christmas cards and envelopes, printed
  Bible verses, Christmas facts from **web ref
  AASA3.Nat_2** for **Bible reading/Game**
- *Showstoppers* DVD or similar video clip to tell part of the
  story for **Bible retelling**
- pictures of four faces for the **Bible talk** – download from
  web ref AASA3.Nat_3
- star-shaped gift tags, pens/pencils for the **Prayer activity**

Beginning the service

With: vox pop resource, downloaded from **web ref AASA3.Nat_1**

Start by playing a vox pop of 'We asked people what Christmas means to them'.. If you don't have access to this, ask members of the congregation to comment on what their friends and neighbours have said to them about Christmas.

Ask the congregation what the most common theme was in the vox pop. They should say 'family'. State that, even though the commercialism of Christmas appears to be increasing, the people's values are still the same as they ever were. They want to spend Christmas at home with those they love.

Emphasise that Christmas is indeed all about family. It is a celebration of when God the Father sent his only Son, Jesus, to earth in order to save us, his children. It is the tale of a parent – God – wanting to spend eternity with the people he loves.

Finish by asking people to talk in twos or threes about what Christmas means to them – not just spiritual topics but the stresses and strains of burning the turkey, experiencing a power cut or being so excited that they can't sleep on Christmas Eve. This will help visitors to feel part of the service.

Bible reading/Game

With: a selection of Christmas cards and coloured envelopes; Christmas facts from **web ref AASA3.Nat_2**; printed Bible verses

Each Bible reading will be preceded by a Christmas card hunt, for all ages to join in. All four readings should be spread throughout the first part of the service, before the **Bible talk**.

Sort the different Christmas cards depicting secular Christmas scenes, eg snowman, Santa, robin, into four groups – at least three per subject. Inside these cards insert the words 'Christmas means…' followed by a seasonal fact, such as 'eating turkey'. You could also include a statistic, eg 'The UK consumes around 10 million turkeys each Christmas.' A list of suggested Christmas facts and statistics can be downloaded; see above.

Also collect four cards that depict the true meaning of Christmas, eg a nativity scene. Inside each 'nativity card', write the words 'Christmas means…' followed by these Bible references:

1) Light coming into the world (John 1:1–18 or Isaiah 9:2–7)

2) God with us (Luke 1:26–38)

3) The birth of Jesus, God's Son (Luke 2:1–7)

4) Celebrating our glorious Saviour (Luke 2:8–20)

Put one of these cards on each of the piles of secular ones and then put each pile in separate, coloured envelopes. There will be one pile for each Bible reading. Alternatively, put the cards in white envelopes marked with different coloured stars or stickers so that it is obvious that they are different. Give the 'nativity' card a mark to distinguish it from the secular ones and number the envelopes so that the envelopes contain the 'nativity' cards in the same order as the Bible verses above. Hide all the cards around the building.

Explain that you're going to have a Christmas card hunt to discover more about the true meaning of Christmas. Invite everyone to search for the first envelope (eg the red one or the starred one). When someone finds an envelope, they should go to the front, where they can be given a prize such as a chocolate.

Ask the 'finder' to open the card and tell everyone what pictures are on the front of it. Then ask them to read what's written inside. Make sure that adults are available to help young children. The 'nativity card' should be read last. After this 'nativity card' has been read, the Bible passage relating to it should be read aloud. To ensure that this is well read, arrange for the reader(s) to be prepared to come to the front when their reading has been found.

Repeat this for all four sets of cards. You could intersperse a carol between at least one of the readings and card hunts, or show the DVD suggested for the **Bible retelling** or light the Advent candle or lead the **Prayer activity.**

Bible retelling

With: *Showstoppers* DVD and suitable equipment to play it

For a refreshing retelling of the Christmas story, play the relevant part of the *Showstoppers* DVD, an SU holiday club DVD (available from Scripture Union). If you don't have this DVD, you could use an alternative video retelling. There is a beautiful clip on YouTube, which tells the story of the nativity to the song 'In My Arms' by Plumb (http://uk.youtube.comwatch?v=rAE2qKXs1Fg). You can also use a clip from www.ignitermedia. com called 'Retooning the Nativity', which strips away some of the human traditions of the nativity. It's quite funny.

Bible talk

With: pictures of four faces, downloaded from **web ref AASA3.Nat_3**

Ask four children to come to help you. Hand each of them a picture of a face. The first child should be given a picture of a 'stressed' face, the second a picture of a 'tired' face, the third child a 'sad' face, and the fourth a picture of a 'happy' face. Ask the children not to show the congregation what face they have received.

Explain that Christmas can mean different things to different people. Ask the first child to hold up the 'stressed' face. People can often get stressed at Christmas-time. The rush to buy presents, food and drink can be too much, and it seems to get more manic every year. Families spend more time with each other at Christmas than at any other time of the year, and this can also, sadly, lead to stresses and strains.

Ask the second child to hold up the 'tired' face. This is what a lot of parents will relate to, particularly mothers! Christmas is often the busiest time of the year. The day starts very early for whoever is cooking the turkey, and hosts barely sit down throughout the whole day – ensuring that their visitors are catered for and have enough to eat and drink. There is the rush to visit friends and family, often travelling long distances. This busyness often means that people return to work in January feeling more tired than they did when they left in December. Children are even glad to go back to school!

Christmas can also be a time of great sadness for some people (ask the third child to hold up the 'sad' face). It can be a time when we remember those whom we have lost – relatives who have died, or friends we have lost touch with. We can find that we ponder on those moments where we have been hurt or rejected by others. Ensure that you are sensitive in this section as there will probably be visitors to your church who will be able to relate to these feelings.

Ask the fourth child to hold up the 'happy' face. Emphasise that there is nothing wrong with people wishing each other 'Merry Christmas', or indulging in traditions such as putting up the tree, eating mince pies or watching *The Snowman*. It is rare for people to be this friendly and joyful, and it is a wonderful thing. However, we need to be

aware of why we celebrate Christmas. Ultimately it is because of the birth of Jesus. Our God came down to earth and that is something to really celebrate. He knew what it was like to be stressed and tired. (Show the first and second faces again.)

But Jesus also came to die a painful and cruel death. He was going to suffer to rescue his children – people who had forgotten about God's love for them. So the sad face has a place in the real Christmas too.

Conclude by expressing your hope that people will put their trust in Jesus this festive season, and wish everybody a happy and peaceful Christmas.

Prayer activity

With: star-shaped gift tags; pens/pencils

Give each person a gift tag and pen or pencil. (Alternatively, these can be handed out at the start of the service as people arrive.) Ask them to think of something they would particularly like to pray for, this Christmas. They may simply want to thank God for sending Jesus. Or they may want to ask him to bring peace to an area of conflict in the world, or to resolve a personal problem.

Encourage them to write or draw their prayer on the gift tag during a time of silence or quiet music. If your church has a Christmas tree, you could invite people to hang their gift tags on it as a way of offering their prayer to God. Or people may prefer to take the gift tags home to hang on their own trees as a reminder.

This is a significant time when people can stop rushing and be still. Draw attention to the importance of finding time for reflection over Christmas. You could encourage parents to build in special times for the whole family to do this – perhaps you could encourage them to use the SU Advent calendar, see page 69.

Prayer of confession

A simple call and response prayer:

Father God, as we rush around buying, wrapping and exchanging gifts this Christmas, we are sorry for the times we forget to thank you for the gift of your precious Son.
Forgive us, we pray.

Lord Jesus, as we spend time celebrating with family and friends this Christmas, we are sorry for the times when we do not think of others and we forget to celebrate your birth.
Forgive us, we pray.

Holy Spirit, as we get swept up in festive parties, decorations and overindulgence this Christmas, we are sorry for the times we forget to invite you to fill us with the true spirit of Christmas. **Forgive us, we pray.**

Ending the service

Finish the service with a rousing carol such as 'Joy to the world', and send people out with a blessing.

You may like to use this prayer by Robert Louis Stevenson:
'Loving Father,
Help us remember the birth of Jesus,
that we may share in the song of the angels,
the gladness of the shepherds,
and worship of the wise men.

Close the door of hate
and open the door of love all over the world.
Let kindness come with every gift
and good desires with every greeting.
Deliver us from evil by the blessing
which Christ brings,
and teach us to be merry with clear hearts.

May the Christmas morning
make us happy to be thy children,
and Christmas evening bring us to our beds
with grateful thoughts,
forgiving and forgiven,
for Jesus' sake.
Amen.'

Notes and comments

Christmas 2008 was the first time that Christians in Nepal could celebrate Christmas. Their Christmas did not have all the commercialism of a western Christmas. To find out more, visit www. biblesociety.org.uk.

Christmas provides an excellent opportunity to reach people who wouldn't normally come to church. You may want to be proactive about this by sending invitations to the local community, letting them know the times of the Christmas services. At the same time, you could inform them of events coming up in the New Year that they might be interested in, such as a new children's club or an Alpha course.

The service itself also provides a good opportunity to talk to people and to make them feel welcome in your church. Invite people to stay for tea and mince pies afterwards, and organise a welcoming team to chat to visitors.

Visitors with young children may feel embarrassed if their children misbehave or are noisy during the service. Make sure they are informed about any crèche facilities or special children's area you have available. You could reassure people at the start that the service is intended for all ages, and that they do not need to worry if children are a bit noisy.

Helpful extras

Music and song ideas

Most people, especially visitors, will expect to sing traditional carols at a Christmas service, and will be disappointed if they don't. So make sure you include some of the following: 'Angels from the realms of glory'; 'Hark! the herald angels sing'; 'Joy to the world'; 'O come, all ye faithful'; 'O little town of Bethlehem'; 'Once in royal David's city'; 'Silent night'.

You could also include a couple of contemporary Christmas songs such as: 'From heaven You came' (*SOF* 120); 'Light of the world' (*SOF* 342) or 'This child' (*ts* 511). The songbook *Carol Praise* (HarperCollins*Publishers*) contains many new carols and reshaped ones.

If your church has a choir or a good vocalist, you could ask them to perform one or two songs as people are arriving.

New Year resolution – Share Jesus!

January

Light series: Travelling in faith
Light readings: Acts 13:1–52; 14:8–28; 16:1–15; 16:16–40

Aims: to begin the new year accepting the challenge to take the good news to the world
to ensure we do this in the way, and go to the places, that Jesus wants

Readings: Genesis 12:1–5; Acts 16:6–10

Getting started

The *Light* material begins the year by looking at the dramatic travels and ministry of Paul and others, with miracles, challenges to local and growing churches, and plenty of opposition from evil spirits and manipulative people! For example, in Lystra, Paul and Barnabas were feted as gods. Paul humbly corrected the people and spoke clearly of the love and power of the true God before being unceremoniously dragged from the town and stoned... quite a visit! It is never going to be easy to share the gospel. The story from Acts 16 that is the focus of this service demonstrates how important it is to share the good news of Jesus, listening to God's prompting through the Spirit. Paul was determined to share the message of Christ as widely as possible, but God's timing and God's plans must be followed.

At the start of a new year, and in the context of intergenerational worship, it is vitally important to grasp the call to share God's message, . We all have a part to play in spreading the word, whether we are young or old. God has a plan and direction for everyone, and he knows when and where it will be most fruitful for us to speak out. May everyone participating in this service be inspired by what God is calling them to be and to do!

You will need:

- displayed photographs and information on mission partners (as appropriate) for **Beginning the service**
- key words for the **Bible talk**, available from **web ref AASA3.Jan_1**
- a small map of the locality or of the world for everyone for **Ending the service**
- a displayed copy of the prayer of response for **Ending the service**, which can be downloaded from **web ref AASA3.Jan_2**

Beginning the service

With: a display of photographs and information about mission partners linked with the church – if the church has broadband and skype, you could even establish live contact.

These people have obeyed God's call at the right time to serve him either in this country or abroad. They will have faced many challenges, but God has directed them and has promised to be with them. Pray for them in small mixed-age groups, prefacing each prayer with 'Thank you, God, that you call people to share the good news. Please... '

Bible reading
Genesis 12:1–5; Acts 16:6–10

The reading below is a combination of both readings, with the congregation making the following response as indicated: **God leads; God provides; God has a plan.** You could display the response on a screen or on the news-sheet.

In the book of Genesis we hear of Abram:
The Lord had said to Abram, 'Leave your country, your people and your father's household and go to the land I will show you.
God leads; God provides; God has a plan.
I will make you into a great nation and I will bless you; I will make your name great, and you will be a blessing.
God leads; God provides; God has a plan.
I will bless those who bless you, and whoever curses you I will curse … '
God leads; God provides; God has a plan. In the book of Acts we hear about Paul:
Paul and his companions travelled throughout the region of Phrygia and Galatia, having been kept by the Holy Spirit from preaching the word in the province of Asia.
God leads; God provides; God has a plan.
When they came to the borders of Mysia, they tried to enter Bithynia, but the Spirit of Jesus would not allow them to.
God leads; God provides; God has a plan.
So they passed by Mysia and went down to Troas.
God leads, God provides, God has a plan.
During the night Paul had a vision of a man of Macedonia standing and begging him, 'Come over to Macedonia and help us.'
God leads; God provides; God has a plan.
After Paul had seen the vision, we got ready at once to leave for Macedonia,
God leads; God provides; God has a plan.
concluding that God had called us to preach the gospel to them.
God leads; God provides; God has a plan.

Bible retelling

This should be done in costume, with the speaker dressed in first-century robes, as befits one of Paul's companions, with clear speech and some movement around the church or worship space.

We've been companions with Paul, who travels all over the place for God. We want to spread the good news of Jesus – that's all that really matters to us!

Paul is determined (I might almost say obsessed) that no one should *not* hear it. So we were really surprised when he said, 'I'm sure the Spirit is telling us not to go to Asia Minor.' OK, so we went along with what he said, but we didn't really understand. We travelled through what you would know as Turkey and had gone all the way north to the borders of Bithynia and were ready to go there. But then Paul said the same thing – the Spirit was stopping him. We want to spread the good news of Jesus – that's all that really matters to us!

I must admit that we began to have real doubts about Paul! We'd been travelling miles, and not gone where we thought we ought to go. Either God had another plan, or Paul had lost it!

Now, I'm not a great one for dreams – as soon as my head touches the pillow I go to sleep, and I don't remember a thing until the next morning. But one night Paul had this dream, and he was sure that in the dream a man from Macedonia was asking for help. That would mean a trip on a boat across the Aegean Sea, heading towards Greece... and I'm not a great sailor!

But God seemed to have it all planned. The people in Macedonia needed to hear about Jesus and we want to spread the good news of Jesus everywhere. And that's all that really matters to us! So… that's where we went.

Bible talk

With: volunteers of all ages to walk with you around the worship space as you talk, from one side, to the middle, ending on the other side; visuals for the three words STOP, GO and SHARE (a download is available from **web ref AASA3. Jan_1**); simple actions for the three words for everyone to copy as they are mentioned; a volunteer to talk about how they share the good news.

STOP
God has called his people, and that includes all of us standing and walking here, and all of you, to spread the good news about Jesus... and we all

know the world needs good news!
God had also called Paul and those with him to spread the gospel. They had wanted to go to what was then known as Asia but God said STOP. (Do the simple STOP action for those with you to copy.) They were going the wrong way. We don't know how God said STOP to Paul – it may have been through a feeling, through clear words, or through someone else's comments. But God said STOP and Paul knew it.

There are times when we have to STOP and do what God says, even if it seems like a good idea to keep going. There's a difference between 'God ideas' and 'good ideas'! It's hard to STOP sometimes – some of us will have lots of energy and want to keep going and keep doing good, but God may want to speak to us, and we need to listen. He may want to say STOP.

GO
Paul and his friends travelled further, and again God said STOP. They wanted to go further north but that was not what God wanted. Then God clearly showed Paul in a dream that it was time to GO. (Do the simple GO action.) They were to go in a boat to Macedonia, and they were to GO as soon as possible in order to help the people there. God said GO and Paul knew it.

There are times when God clearly says GO to us. He may do that through others, through the Bible, through circumstances and through prayer. God may want us to GO to school or work and talk about how good church is or to share what Jesus means to us. God may want us to GO to a different part of the world as our linked missionaries have or change where or how we live. Paul knew he had to GO, and in the Old Testament Abram was told to GO, and he did. God blessed both Abraham and Paul. It can be scary to GO where God sends us, but God really does know best!

SHARE
Paul and his friends had learned to STOP when God told them to, and had heard God say GO and had gone! But why did God send them over the sea to Macedonia, closer to Greece? God sent them to SHARE the good news of Jesus, and SHARE with everyone there that God loved them. (Do the simple SHARE action.)

Wherever we GO and whatever we do, we should take every opportunity to SHARE the good news of Jesus. The worship we give God in church should be the same as our lives outside church as we SHARE how Jesus cares about us. We can do that in lots of ways, and at any age. Children and young people can be brilliant as they SHARE about Jesus with their friends, if they let God help them. And how many adults really take every chance God gives to GO and SHARE at work or in other places? In this new year, God is saying to us:

- STOP avoiding what God is saying to us
- GO to where God is calling us
- SHARE God's love with others.

How will you respond? At this point, ask someone to talk appropriately about how they have responded to God's call to share their faith with a friend, family member or colleague, or share a positive story about an Alpha (or similar) course.

Prayer activity
With: pieces of paper and pens; quiet worship music/Taizé song; use the same simple actions you used during the **Bible talk**

Play quiet worship music, or a CD of the Taizé song, 'O Lord, hear my prayer' while you do this. Hand out paper and pens. Ask everyone to think about a time when God has said STOP to them, or think of something that God may want them to STOP doing. Ask everyone to write or draw this on part of the paper. Children may need some help. Then encourage the use of the STOP action as you say:

Dear God, help us to STOP when you tell us to. Help us to STOP doing things that are wrong.

Ask everyone to think of a time when God said GO, or think of places that they go to regularly such as school, work or community venues. Everyone should write or draw these things on the paper. Use the GO action as you pray:

Dear God, help us to GO where you want us to GO, and help us to hear you when you challenge us to GO somewhere new.

Ask everyone to think about opportunities to SHARE their faith with others and the good news that Jesus loves them. Everyone should either draw or write the name of one person they could SHARE the gospel with. Use the action for SHARE as you pray:

Dear God, help us to SHARE the great news of your love with anyone we can, and especially with those we have thought about today.

Prayer of confession
Encourage everyone to say together to God:
Lord of all goodness, forgive us.

Lord of all goodness, forgive us
for the times we have not listened to you.
Lord of all goodness, forgive us
for the times we have gone on without your
guidance.
Lord of all goodness, forgive us
for the times when we have not stopped to listen.
Lord of all goodness, forgive us
for the times we have not gone your way.
Lord of all goodness, forgive us
For the times we have refused to go.
Lord of all goodness, forgive us
for the times we have not shared your gospel.
Lord of all goodness, forgive us
for the times we have denied our faith.
Lord of all goodness, forgive us
and make us into people who listen, and who
share.

Prayer response

Ask people to stand in small groups in a circle
with their backs facing the rest of the group. Each
group will need space around them. Remind them
of the challenges and hardships that Paul faced
doing God's work, but also remind them that he
had companions who travelled with him. We serve
God with others. (You could remind them of the
second outline in this book and 2 Corinthians 12:9.)

Ask everyone to close their eyes. Explain that
anyone who is willing to share Jesus with others,
should take a step forward. Pray for all those who
have stepped forward, that God will strengthen
them.

Ask everyone to turn to face the front (the circles
are broken) and only then open their eyes. Take
hold of someone's hand. Thank God that we
belong to each other and can support each other
as we share Jesus.

Provide the option for people to receive prayer
at the end of the service, if they made a significant
step of commitment.

Ending the service

With: a small map for everyone (of your locality
or of the world); the prayer of response displayed
– also available as a download from **web ref
AASA3.Jan_2**

God wants us all to take the good news to
wherever in the world he has called us to be, or
to go. We may not know the places and situations
God is calling us to, and we may not know when
he will tell us to go. As you hold this map in your
hand, say this prayer by repeating each line:
We will GO where you lead us.
We will STOP when you tell us.

We will SHARE all your love for us.
Lead us, show us and help us.

Helpful extras

Music and song ideas
'O Lord, hear my prayer' (Taizé *SOF* 423);
'One shall tell another' (*SOF* 439); 'Will you
follow the shepherd' (*ks2* 785); 'Rejoice!'
(*SOF* 480); 'Make way, make way' (*ks* 249);
'For I'm building a people of power' (*ks* 61);
'Go, go, go' (*ks* 90); 'Children of the world'
from *LFE* CD (SU)

Game
Where do I go? God may want us to go to
different places and situations to share the
message of the good news. Here are some
examples. Split the congregation into two teams,
and in turn ask them to guess the place by giving
one clue at a time. Award most points for the
fewer clues they need to guess the place.
Hospital: lots of beds/people are treated there/
doctors and nurses
School: sometimes noisy/people learn there/
teachers and children
Park: usually green/things to play on/paths, and
people walking dogs
Supermarket: lots of shelves/things to buy/
trolleys and checkouts
Seaside: water and land/children playing/sand,
stones and sea

Notes and comments

You may want to place more emphasis on what
the church is going to do at the start of the
new year to share the message of Christ. The
Methodist Covenant service is often used as a
basis for this. You could review plans for the year
ahead and use that as a basis of prayer. Focus on
and pray for people who are going away from
your church to settle elsewhere, or who have
changed jobs, schools or roles in some way.

Consider as a church whether there are any
areas or places in the church community where
church people, of any age, do not go. Prayerfully
consider how the church could reach those areas
in practical and spiritual ways. Be open to God's
STOP and GO! Look out for any evangelistic
initiatives that are taking place or being promoted
in your area, and consider whether your church
could get on board with them.

If you are using *The All-age Service Annual Volume
Three* throughout the year, you will encounter Paul
again in the 14th service outline, as he meets the
leaders of the church in Ephesus.

God is so generous

February

Light series: Life in the desert
Light readings: Selected verses from Exodus 16, 19, 20, 33, 34, 35, 36, 39, 40

Aims: to discover the story of the bitter water following on from the praiseful
song of Moses
to recognise that God provides for his people generously

Readings: Exodus 15:1–27; John 4:3–14

Getting started

In February 2010, _Light_ looks at God's generous love and care. He had rescued his people from slavery
and oppression in Egypt and brought them to freedom through the exodus. The Bible reading in Exodus
15 follows on from the miraculous crossing of the Red Sea. The people's immediate grumbling and
complaining is in striking contrast to God's stunning favours given to them in the exodus itself, and in
contrast to their initial response in the song of praise. Yet God still generously pours out favour towards
them, just as true now as then!

The _Light_ material continues the story by looking at later episodes during the wilderness wanderings
which show God's continuing generosity. The people grumble about the food and God sends manna
and quail. God has already saved his people but then he goes further and gives them his words, the
commandments, showing how to live life to the full. He then goes further still by revealing to Moses his
presence and glory.

Perhaps after the exhilaration of Christmas and New Year, when there was so much promise and a sense
of renewal we too have lost our enthusiasm and gratitude. May the people at this service grab hold of
the truth that God persists with us, with overwhelming generosity.

You will need:

- a bulb and dying remains of spring flowers for **Beginning the service**
- Exodus 15:1–21 – download **web ref AASA3.Feb_1**, with props, for the **Bible reading**
- Exodus 15:22–27 with slides – download **web ref AASA3.Feb_2**, for the **Bible talk**
- John 4:3–14 as a script – download **web ref AASA3.Feb_3**, for the **Bible reading**
- the stained glass image of Jesus meeting the woman at the well – download **web ref AASA3.
  Feb _5**, for the **Bible reading**
- three cardboard boxes and their contents for the **Bible talk**
- bowl of water for **Prayers of confession**
- **Statement of faith** – download **web ref AASA3.Feb_4**

Beginning the service

With: a bulb; dying remains of some spring flowers

We are surrounded by a God who gives generously through the natural world he has made. Hold up a plant bulb and the dead spring flowers. Throughout the year, this pattern will be repeated as we sow tiny seeds and harvest vast crops of vegetables. God is a generous giver. Today we will learn how God showed his generosity in the history of his people.

Bible reading
Exodus 15:1–27

Give the background to the reading of the first part of Exodus 15:1–27. It is effective if the four readers have amplification and have practised. 'Voice 1' is the narrator; 'Voice 4' needs to be female (Miriam). The rest of the verses are split between the other two voices. 'Voice 3' stands at some distance from 'Voice 2', to echo the key truths. A trumpet fanfare, a drum roll or a clash of cymbals heralds the start of the reading and establishes a celebratory tone. The reading is also available as a download from **web ref AASA3. Feb_1**.

Exodus 15:22–27 can be used at the start of the **Bible talk** with a slide accompaniment, which is available as a download – **web ref AASA3. Feb_2**.

John 4:3–14
The Gospel reading can be acted (rather than read, as in the Old Testament reading above) with a narrator, Jesus and the Samaritan woman. The setting could be by the font or baptistery (if you have one), which acts as the well. The actors do not have to be dressed up in period costume. God's truth is for us in the 21st century. John 4:3–14 as a script is available as a download from **web ref AASA3.Feb_3**. During this reading you could show the stained glass image of Jesus meeting the woman at the well, which is available as a download from **web ref AASA3.Feb_5**.

Bible talk

With: slides to illustrate Exodus 15:22–27, downloadable from **web ref AASA3.Feb_2**; three cardboard boxes decorated with wrapping paper (graduated sizes to suggest God being more and more generous): inside the first have a bottle containing cloudy water, inside the second, a bottle of clear water and a piece of branch or twig; inside the third, 12 bottles of clear water; if the reading from John 4 is used, a bottle of still water and a bottle of aerated water

Begin by referring to Exodus 15:1–21. Ask why the people were so happy, so full of song (because God had delivered them from Egypt). But hear what happens just a very short time later! The rest of Exodus 15:22–27 should now be read to the accompaniment of a series of slides: verse 22: Picture of desert; verse 23: Symbol for water 'Not drinkable'; verse 24: Silhouette of people arguing; verse 25: Picture of a piece of wood; verse 26: Picture of an ear; verse 27: Picture of fertile oasis with palm trees. Or you could use the download.

We all have received generous gifts, perhaps for Christmas or birthdays. But so easily we forget and we can soon seem ungrateful to the giver. God had led his people out of Egypt into the desert and to freedom. They felt exhilarated. But the sense of joy soon wore off. They were out in the desert. Human beings are made of 60 per cent water. They need water to cope with the heat; so, just three days after the escape from Egypt, God led them to water at a place called Marah.

The yukky water
Open the first smallest box and show the bottle of water. The people started to complain that this water didn't taste right. 'Don't like this.' 'Yuk!' 'I wouldn't have come if I'd known.' This was just days, only *three* days, after the people had been led out of Egypt, to freedom! This was three days after they had worshipped God, singing, 'Who is like you … working wonders?' The water was water. It was not poisonous. It just didn't taste how they wished.

The sweetened water
So God was even more generous. Open the second box, which has the piece of wood. God instructed Moses how to make the water taste sweeter. He told him to take a piece of wood (perhaps a herb) and throw it into the water. Show the clear water. In all this, God did not threaten his people. He was behaving in a generous manner. After this episode, God led the people on to another oasis at Elim. This was only six or seven miles further on.

The quality 'spa' water
Open the third box, the largest one, and show the 12 bottles of water. What confirms God's care for his people is that here at this oasis, there was not one but 12 springs. There were 70 palm trees growing to prove that there were no hidden problems with this water.

The *Light* theme has emphasised God's continuing

generosity. He supplies not only water, but food, with the manna and quail. He not only rescues his people but provides them with the Ten Commandments to enable them to get the most from life.

(An optional second **Bible talk**)
The story from John 4 confirms God's generosity. The woman had come to a well to fetch water. Jesus goes a step further and offers her not just still water but fresh running water: not just water for today but water for eternal life. A bottle of still water contrasted with a bottle of aerated water can represent this difference. In the bubbly water there is more life and fizz and sparkle. A couple of children could be asked to taste and contrast the two drinks of water.

This is how Christians experience God. He is far more generous to us than we deserve or expect. At this point, a member of the church could talk about how God has been generous to them time and again. This needs to be prepared and a planned question and answer session would ensure that the focus is on the key theme of generosity. It could focus on prayer requests and how these have been answered abundantly. The person being interviewed could describe how God has shaped their life and given so much more than they ever expected.

At the end, listen to 'I will say' by Lou Fellingham. The words can be displayed on a screen. This song combines ideas from both readings. It includes 'I will say of the Lord, He is my strength' (Exodus 15:2) and 'I will drink of the well that never dries' (John 4:13,14). These links need to be explained.

Prayer of confession

Water should be poured into a bowl. Read the following confession so that people can think if this is what they want to say to God; then the congregation should repeat each line after the leader.

Lord, you give us water to drink.
You give us water to wash ourselves clean.
You generously forgive us.
Take away all that stains us.
Remove the dirt from our lives.
Make us fit to live in your presence.
Amen

Prayers of intercession

With: the slides used for the reading of Exodus 15:22–27 – **web ref AASA3.Feb_2** – as a visual focus for intercessions

Three people can take two sections each. After the first five sections, 'O Lord, hear my prayer' can be sung. After the sixth, 'The Lord is my song'.

1) Desert
Lord, we bring before you the desert places of the world, and the desert places of our lives. Bring the water of life to them.

2) 'Not drinkable'
Lord, we pray for those who are short of water, and those short of pure water. We ask for your protection and guidance for those charities that bring wells, pumps and running water.

3) Silhouette of people arguing
Lord, help us to say 'thank you' and to live in peace with one another and with you.

4) Piece of wood
Lord, you transform situations. Change hatred to love. Turn war to peace. Take away bitterness and change situations to sweetness.

5) Ear
Lord, thank you for giving us your word, your commandments, and teachers to help us. May we listen and learn from your truth.

6) Desert oasis
Lord, we praise you for the beauty and wealth of creation. You are a generous God. Give us generous hearts we pray, in Jesus' name. Amen

Ending the service

Moses and the people saw God's kindness. He generously brought them out of slavery in Egypt. He led them to water, transformed the bitter water to sweet, and then took them to an oasis with 12 springs. His kindness never ends. He was their song; he was their source of joy. He is our song. He is our source of joy. The service should end with music playing or everyone singing, 'The Lord is my song' or 'Shout for joy and sing'.

Helpful extras

Music and song ideas

Introductory songs of celebration, for example 'Shout for joy and sing' (ts 450); at the end of the **Bible talk**, 'I will say' by Lou Fellingham (from *Treasure* CD); to develop the idea of our thirst for water supplied by God, 'As water to the thirsty' (*SOF* 659); 'As the deer pants for the water' (*SOF* 658); 'Have you heard the raindrops?' (ks 99); 'I heard the voice of Jesus say' (*SOF* 215) describes Jesus as 'that life-giving stream'.

To use during intercessions, 'Longing for light' (*Spring Harvest* 2005) which refers to those 'longing for water'; two Taizé songs: 'O Lord, hear my prayer' and 'The Lord is my song', which pick up the ideas from Exodus 15:2 that the Lord is our song, and from John 4 that he is 'the well-spring of life'.

To highlight the theme of generosity, 'Now thank we all our God' (*SOF* 405); 'Great is thy faithfulness' (*SOF* 147); 'Who is like you?' (*Up to Zion* Hosanna Music CD); 'He supplies' (*Bitesize Bible Songs 2* CD, SU)

Statement of faith

Available as a download – **web ref AASA3. Feb_4** – and based on Exodus 15, this can be said in two parts either with a leader and the congregational response or with two halves of the congregation taking the two parts.

Notes and comments

Because music and song have an additional importance in the Old Testament reading, this could be an opportunity publicly to thank the musicians. At the very least, they could be given a written thank you in private. Music could be accompanied by tambourines and other percussion instruments.

Oriel in the Desert by Robert Harrison (SU, pages 173–175) gives an imaginative retelling of this exodus episode from an archangel's point of view.

Fire by night by Hannah MacFarlane (Scripture Union) is a dramatic account of the exodus, retold for 8–11s. For this service, you could read Chapters 21 and 23. They are only four pages and two pages long. For more details of this book see page 15.

Resources for Easter

Great gifts to give to young children in an all-age service or in a toddler group while *The Big Yellow Book* is full of Easter ideas to use with under fives.

Happy Easter
978 1 84427 226 6
75p

My Little Yellow Book
978 1 85999 693 5
£3.50

The Big Yellow Book
978 1 85999 692 8
£9.99

Easter Cracked
978 1 84427 189 4 **£9.99**

Celebrations Sorted
978 1 84427 182 X **£9.99**

Resource books packed full of craft, drama, all-age services and more, to use in Easter celebrations and throughout the year (such as at Harvest or Pentecost).

Top Tips on Explaining the Cross to Children and Young People
978 1 84427 330 0 **£2.99**
Top Tips on Helping a child respond to Jesus 978 1 84427 387 4 **£2.99**

Two titles in this essential series of short books to enable you to explain the meaning of the cross and resurrection to children (and people of all ages) and our response to it. Full of inspirational stories and practical advice!

Fiction titles

Belcher Bridget
978 1 84427 337 9
£3.99

All these books, beautifully written and illustrated by Alexander Brown, explore four gospel parables. Ideal as gifts or to use for reading in an all-age service. *Belcher Bridget* is available as a PowerPoint to be used with service outline 13, **web ref AASA3.Aug_1** (see page 114).

Brilliant Bones
978 1 84427 263 1
£3.99

Anthony Greenfinger's Apple Disaster
978 1 84427 262 4
£3.99

Mrs O'Brady Never Gives Up
978 1 84427 338 6
£3.99

Holiday and midweek club material

Look out for the new holiday club programme *Rocky's Plaice*, with the *Rocky's Plaice* DVD and *Rocky's Menu*. *Takeaway* is the eyelevel midweek club programme, which builds on this, but it can be used as a stand-alone programme, aimed specifically at unchurched children.

Showstoppers
978 1 84427 343 0 **£9.99**

Showstoppers DVD
978 1 84427 344 7
£19.99

Showstoppers Cast List (Single)
978 1 84427 345 3 **£1.99**
(Packs of 10)
978 1 84427 346 1 **£10.00**

This holiday club programme is based around five of the key 'Must Know' Bible stories that must be passed on to the next generation. Each story is presented by the children, using drama, music, mime and art in a grand showtime finale. The programme contains everything you need to run a holiday club programme.

Dress rehearsal 978 1 84427 383 6 **£9.99**
Dress rehearsal DVD 978 1 84427 393 5 **£14.99**

The eyelevel midweek club programme builds on *Showstoppers* but can be used as a stand-alone programme, aimed specifically at unchurched children. The programme explores eight stories including five more of the key 'Must Know' Bible stories. There is plenty of dressing up and preparing for a 'Showtime' at the end of each session.

Prices are correct at the time of going to print. All are available from good Christian bookshops or Scripture Union Mail Order or online – www.scriptureunion.org.uk/shop

These are other programmes to use in an eyelevel midweek club.

Awesome
978 1 84427 153 5
£9.99

Streetwise
978 1 85999 767 3
£9.99

Clues2Use
978 1 84427 113 9
£9.99

Rocky Road
978 1 84427 183 2
£9.99

Target Challenge
978 1 84427 314 0
£9.99

High Five
978 1 84427 251 8
£9.99

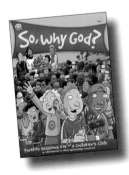

So, why God?
978 1 84427 222 8
£9.99

Shining like stars

March

Light series: Light for life
Light readings: Psalm 119:9–16,105; Proverbs 22:22–25; 23:1–5; John 9:1–12,35–38; 8:12; Matthew 5:14–16

Aims: to explore what Paul meant when he urged the Philippians to be different, to be light
to accept the challenge to shine for God even though it may be tough

Readings: Philippians 2:14–16; 1 Kings 19:9–15

Getting started

In March 2010 *Light* explores the theme of light. The series looks at how, in a dark world, God's Word is light showing us the way to live. It reflects on Jesus himself, 'the Light of the world', who brings life-changing light into our lives. And then, amazingly, we discover how God calls us to shine as light for him in our twisted, suffering world, so that others – at school, at home (get ready for Mothering Sunday!), at work – can be changed.

In this service, which complements the series, we hear from the apostle Paul. Writing from the darkness of prison and facing possible execution, he encourages believers at Philippi to keep on shining 'like stars' for Jesus. Sometimes, we may feel, as Elijah did, as if we're the 'only one' who is living for God (which wasn't even true for Elijah). Like Paul, safe in God's light, we must keep on shining.

'Light' is a challenging theme. We'll need to make sure that the examples and language we use are appropriate to both younger and older members of our congregation. So, as Easter draws near, let's take up the lamp of God's Word, come close to Jesus the Light, and share that light with those around us – as we meet in fresh ways with God who is Light.

You will need:

- PowerPoint slide show – which can be downloaded from **web ref AASA3.Mar_1** (to be used on several occasions) plus additional images and sound effects, and stars and candles, for **Beginning the service**, **Prayers of intercession** and **Ending the service**
- **Bible retelling** download – **web ref AASA3.Mar_4**
- a labelled large box with contents for the **Bible talk**
- the words of the **Prayer of confession** from **web ref AASA3. Mar_6**

Beginning the service

Aim to create an atmosphere in your meeting place which introduces the theme of the service: shining like stars. Do this in the following ways:

- As people are entering, display on a loop the downloadable PowerPoint slide show **web ref AASA3.Mar_1**. Slide 2 shows a picture of stars in a night sky with the words 'Shine like stars' (Philippians 2:15)
- Lower the main lights and, against dark backgrounds (eg a dark area, or black sugar paper on walls), display or suspend on thread some cut out shining stars. You could pick out some of these with spotlights, using carefully placed torches or small lamps. For instructions for making stars see **web ref AASA3.Mar_2**.
- Burn a large candle at the front of your seating area to provide a focus and a reminder that Jesus is the 'Light of the world' (John 8:12).
- As the congregation arrives, give everyone two star-shaped cards (one foil-backed; one white or coloured, on which they can write). Also, hand out candles to every person.

At the start, pause the PowerPoint loop. Freeze on Slide 2, with stars in the night sky. Welcome everyone and ask if anyone can guess the theme of the service. Answers will probably include words such as 'stars', 'light', 'shining'. Briefly comment that Jesus called himself the Light of the world and now he wants us to share his light with others. Paul said that, as God's people, we should 'shine like stars'.

To help everyone to start thinking about what that means, ask them to take the foil-backed star and stick or hang it up with thread around the meeting area. When everyone is sitting down again, say that God wants us to shine like stars in a world which often seems dark and difficult.

Bible reading
Philippians 2:14–16

Explain that you are going to hear from Paul's letter to Christians at Philippi (in modern-day Greece). When he wrote these words, he was a prisoner, in chains in Rome. Even so, he was witnessing to those around him and encouraging others through writing letters. He was shining like a star in dark places.

Ask a number of volunteers to prepare this reading as indicated below, leaving a pause after each section. Position the readers around your meeting area so that the congregation hears each phrase coming from different places. If more light is needed for reading, ask individual readers to use a small torch shining on their Bible verses. This passage is also available as a download from **web ref AASA3.Mar_3**.

During the pauses, invite everyone to think about each phrase and ask themselves what God might be saying to them.

Read Philippians 2:14–16 (CEV):

Verse 14: Do everything without grumbling or arguing.
Verse 15a: Then you will be the pure and innocent children of God.
Verse 15b: You live among people who are crooked and evil …
Verse 15c: … but you must not do anything that they can say is wrong.
Verse 15d: Try to shine as lights among the people of this world …
Verse 16a: … as you hold firmly to the message that gives life.
Verse 16b: Then on the day when Christ returns, I can take pride in you.
Verse 16c: I can also know that my work and efforts were not useless.

At the end of the reading, allow a few moments for quiet prayerful reflection.

Bible retelling
1 Kings 19:9–15

For a dramatic retelling of the story of Elijah on the mountain go to **web ref AASA3.Mar_4**. Additional visual and sound effects are available from **web ref AASA3.Mar_5** and **7**. Elijah learned the hard way what it meant to shine as a light for God. If you choose to use this retelling, continue with it straight after the Philippians reading.

Bible talk

With: a large box with comments such as 'Open with care' or 'Will change your life' written on it in large letters, and a Bible inside - place torches inside the box so that, as it is opened, light will shine out; image of Jesus on the cross or as the Light of the world – see **web ref AASA3.Mar_1**

This talk focuses on Philippians 2:14–16.

Shine like stars
Display Slide 2 (stars in the night sky) from the PowerPoint slide show. Comment briefly on some of the ideas seen earlier in the slide show, explaining how each tells us something about how

we are to be light for Jesus, or how he is light. Ask how we can shine like stars for Jesus in our world – especially when things are difficult and we feel we're on our own. (If you used the second service outline on the tough situation Moses found himself in, from Exodus 5 and 6, refer to this.) Interview two or three volunteers to find out how they are trying to serve God in situations that are sometimes difficult, for example:

- leaders from your church – youth or children's worker, home group leader
- a young person trying to live for God at school
- someone who is trying to live for God at work
- a mother of young children
- someone who is ill or elderly
- someone with a dramatic story of how they have kept on living for God in spite of difficult circumstances

How can we shine like stars?

- **No complaining or arguing** (Philippians 2:14)
  Ask for a show of hands. Has anyone complained (aloud or in their heads) or argued today? Light-heartedly acknowledge that you have complained too – (about burnt toast, the cat etc!). Point out that it's hard to live as God wants.

- **Live the good life**
  Jesus says we are the light of the world (Matthew 5:14) – we reflect his light. We need to be different as we deliberately choose to do what's right and good. Amazingly, Jesus says that as we do this, others will turn to God (Matthew 5:14–16; Philippians 2:15,16).

- **Hold on to God's Word** (Philippians 2:16)
  Bring out the large box. What might be inside? Ask for a young volunteer who is brave enough to open it. Create a sense of excitement and nervous anticipation as you encourage your volunteer to open the box. Bring out the Bible which is inside.

  The Bible isn't just an old book. It is God's Word – and it's powerful. It will change us and is described as light to help us to live God's way (Psalm 119:9–16,105). It also contains the good news about Jesus, which God wants us to share with others so that they can come to know him and be changed too (Philippians 2:16).

  Briefly challenge everyone that if we want to shine for Jesus, it's very important that we listen to him by reading the Bible.

- **You're not on your own**
  Elijah thought he was 'the only one' (1 Kings

19:10,14). It seemed as though everything had gone wrong and there was no hope. Yet, he discovered that God was with him.
Jesus has called us to be lights to the world, because he is 'the light of the world' (John 8:12). We're not asked to 'shine' on our own. We can turn to Jesus, who will not only transform the dark things in our lives but wants us, as his representatives, to bring his light to others.

- **God is pleased with you**
  Paul knew living for Jesus wasn't easy. He makes it clear that he would be proud of those who would follow his teaching and shine for God (Philippians 2:16). And God will be pleased with us too as we, with determination and courage, shine for him.

So, are you shining for Jesus?

End with a challenge.
- Where has God placed you to shine for him?
- Does your living and life bring light to those places?
- Do others notice that you are different?
- Are you offering 'the word of life' to others?
- Does the light of your life show others the way to Jesus?

Prayers of confession

Display Image 5, the Light of the world from the PowerPoint slide. Allow a few minutes of quiet for people to focus on the image of Jesus. Invite everyone to quietly name before God any ways in which they have *not* been 'shining stars' in recent days. Then say the prayer of confession together and use **web ref AASA3.Mar_6**. This could either be displayed on a screen, printed on a separate sheet, or included on the news-sheet.

Prayers of intercession

With: the non-foil stars that were given out as people arrived; pens; the prayer

Ask everyone to take the other star they were given and write on it a situation that needs God's light. Invite people in twos or threes to talk about what they have written down – for example, a world or local issue, situations in the church, someone who does not know Jesus, people who are ill, personal situations. In silence or out loud, pray for one another, for the situation and for courage and wisdom as you go out to be light in the world.

Close this time with this prayer which comes from the *Book of Common Prayer*, 1662. Comment that it is a prayer that Christians have been saying to God for almost three hundred and fifty years, asking for God to give them his light and protection! It can be downloaded from **web ref AASA3.Mar_8**.

Lighten our darkness, we beseech thee, O Lord; and by thy great mercy defend us from all perils and dangers of this night; for the love of thy only Son, our Saviour Jesus Christ. Amen.

Encourage everyone to take their star home and put it where they'll see it often, as a reminder to pray that the light of Jesus will shine in the world and through their lives.

Ending the service

With: a candle for each person, given out as people arrive; PowerPoint slides from **web ref AASA3.Mar_1**

Keep on display the PowerPoint slide with the image of Jesus as the Light of the world. Light a few candles and ask everyone to share their light. Emphasise the need for great care!

As the lighting of the candles takes place, run the PowerPoint slide show again with some suitable music playing quietly in the background (eg 'Shine, Jesus, shine'). At the same time, several volunteers can read aloud three or four of the following verses as appropriate, leaving pauses for reflection in between each. As earlier in the service, readers could be positioned around the building, so that the words come from different angles. End with the PowerPoint slide showing stars in a dark sky and the words: 'Shine like stars'.

The verses are: John 8:12; 1 Kings 19:11,12; Isaiah 9:2; Luke 2:29–32; Matthew 5:14–16; Philippians 2:14–16a; Revelation 3:20

Close the service with the blessing from Numbers 6:24–26. Make sure all candles are extinguished before everyone starts to move about.

Helpful extras

Notes and comments

Make the theme evident in everything that happens – visually, in words and actions – from the moment people enter the service (see **Beginning the service**).

As some preparation is needed, check through the material to make sure you have everything you need.

Those involved in the **Bible reading** and **Bible retelling** will need to prepare. Omit the Bible retelling (Elijah on the mountain) if there isn't time in your service (**web ref AASA3.Mar_4**). If you decide to omit the Elijah retelling, explain briefly in the **Bible talk** about this part of Elijah's story.

If some of the more technical things are not possible in your situation, use your imagination and adapt as needed.

We pray that this service will help you and your congregation to meet with Jesus, the Light, and encourage you as you seek to share his light with others.

Home is a place where...

Mothering Sunday

Aim: to engage with the time when Jesus entered the home of Simon Peter to celebrate the family and home as a place of healing, service and welcome, where Jesus is invited in

Readings: Mark 1:29–34; Colossians 3:12–21

Getting started

The story of Jesus healing Simon's mother-in-law is the focus of this service. Mothering Sunday can be painful for many people, so this service focuses on the whole family – all generations – and the home as a place of healing, service and welcome, where Jesus is invited in – a very suitable theme for an all-age service!

This healing on the Sabbath was itself a challenge to the authorities. Jesus was likely to encounter the wrath of the religious leaders, so it is a clear demonstration of the depth of his compassion. Nothing was going to stop him from doing his duty – not even the socially accepted behaviour of the day. It is also interesting to note that this healing took place in private. Jesus wasn't interested in showing off or being a hero – he simply met people's needs wherever he encountered them (although his miracles were a public sign of who he was and the nature of his mission).

This account of Jesus' miracle in a domestic setting fits comfortably into the Colossians passage, which gives practical instructions for family life. Paul gives guidelines to the Colossian church, both for living as a community of Christians and for living within their individual families. In the new life we share with Christ, each person has a role and responsibility to fulfil.

You will need:

- several large cardboard boxes and flowers for **Beginning the service**
- actors to mime for the **Bible retelling** – download **web ref AASA3.Moth_3**
- a recording about four children's chosen relative and four envelopes with cards for the **Bible talk**
- pencils and rectangles of coloured paper for the **Prayer activity**
- download **web ref AASA3.Moth_1** for **Ending the service**

Beginning the service

With: several large cardboard boxes; flowers

Before the service, gather together several empty cardboard boxes. On one box, write the words 'Supported by God' and place the flowers inside this box. On each of the other boxes, write the name of someone who makes up a household, eg mother, child, father, grandparent, lodger or a pet.

Place the 'Supported by God' box on a firm base in clear view of the congregation, with the words at the back so they cannot be seen. Talk about the households in which we live and who might be found in them. As each member of the household is mentioned, show the box with that name on it, and gradually build them on top of the first box to make a tower.

When the final box has been added, pretend to realise that you have mislaid something important and say that it must be in the bottom box. Enlist someone from the congregation to help you remove that one from the pile. Ask them to ease the box out while you hold on to the rest. Predictably, this will end in disaster with all the boxes collapsing. Only the box at the foot of the tower will remain.

Now turn this box around to show the congregation the words: 'Supported by God'. Say that this statement is true in two senses. Firstly, God is a great supporter of families. He longs to see them enjoying their shared life. Secondly, if God gets pushed out of a family's life, they lose the most effective means of support in both bad times and good.

Open the last box to reveal the flowers inside. Share how God gives us individuals in our lives to support us and care for us. Invite the children to collect a flower to give to their mum or someone else who cares for them. Encourage everyone else who wants to thank someone who supports them to come forward to collect a flower.

As a light-hearted way to introduce the service, there is a drama script entitled *Some kids do 'ave 'em!* available as a download from **web ref AASA3.Moth_2**. Comment that families are all different but we all have to get on together, which means serving one another and making allowances for each other. This is illustrated in the Bible story in this service.

Bible reading

Before reading Colossians 3:12–21 (preferably from the CEV), teach the congregation the following actions when they hear the following words:

'Love' – they should draw a heart shape in the air.
'Each other' – they should point to everyone around them.
'Together' – they should hold hands with the person next to them.
'Lord' – they should raise their arms up to the sky.

This is a simple but effective way to bring the passage to life. Remember that people of all ages can join in with the actions – not just the children!

Mark 1:29–34 should also be read aloud, and could be followed by the sketch in **Bible retelling**.

Bible retelling

The script is a version of Mark 1:29–34, taken from *LightLive* and is available as a download from **web ref AASA3.Moth_3**. Prepare one person to read the script as narrated by Simon's mother-in-law and four actors to mime Jesus, Simon, Simon's wife and Simon's mother-in-law. Invite five volunteers (possibly children) to be the townspeople. They should each think of an imaginary ailment they are suffering from. Ask them to sit near the front, listen for their cue and mime appropriately. Everyone else should imagine they are living in towns and villages all over Galilee.

Introduce the reader as a lady living at the time of Jesus, preferably a mature woman, dressed in biblical clothes. The scene starts with just the mother-in-law on stage, lying down as if ill.

Bible talk

With: a recording of four children talking about someone in their family; four envelopes each containing a card on which is written one of these phrases: 'A place of healing'; 'A place of service'; 'A place of welcome'; 'A place where Jesus is invited'

Before the service, find four children who are willing to be recorded talking about someone in their family who will be at church on Mothering Sunday. Choose carefully, so as not to put any families under pressure, and make sure you have permission from one of the adults in the household to do this.

When you record the children, ask them to describe what their relation looks like, what they enjoy most about them, what their good points are and so on. Make sure they don't reveal the name of the person being described! Keep all comments positive and don't let the interview drag on for too long (30 or 40 seconds is the ideal length for each interview). During the talk, you should play the recordings in turn and ask the person who is being described in each to come forward when they recognise themselves. Enjoy the surprise and laughter.

A place of healing
Explain what you have done; then play the first interview. When the first person comes forward, give them the first envelope. Explain that inside is one of the four good things about family life as described in the **Bible reading**. Ask this person to open the envelope and read the card aloud. It says: 'A place of healing'. Comment on all the people who cared for Simon's mother-in-law and helped her back to health. Ask your unexpected assistant whether they can remember a time when someone in the family was unwell and the rest of the family helped out. You might get a one-word reply or an anecdote – either way, congratulate your helper on what they have said. Encourage everyone to try to make their home a place where care and love are offered to those in need.

A place of service
Play the second interview, resulting in the second person coming forward. This time, the feature of good family life contained in the envelope is: 'A place of service'. Remind everyone that Simon's mother-in-law was so grateful for being well again that she wanted to serve everyone a meal. She already had the role of one who served others. Ask your helper to recall a recent time when someone in their family was helpful to someone else.

A place of welcome
Continue in the same way. The third interview will bring to the front someone who will read out the card saying: 'A place of welcome'. Point out that the whole town was made welcome at Simon's house in order to meet Jesus, and ask whether your helper ever has guests to visit their home. Comment that hospitality is one of the expected characteristics of God's community and can take many different forms. Do comment that 'hospitality' does not just mean someone staying for a week, or even coming for a meal. Welcoming someone for a drink or even being generous with time and interest is all part of being hospitable.

A place where Jesus is invited
Play the final interview. The fourth envelope should contain a card which says: 'A place where

Jesus is invited'. Explain that all these good things happened because Jesus was asked into the home. Ask your final guest about a time when their family really felt the presence of Jesus in their household.

Thank all those who have taken part, and assure everyone of the care that Jesus has for their family. It would be very appropriate to thank God for the families of those in the church and to ask God to help them to exhibit these characteristics, taking them one at a time.

Prayer activity
With: pencils; rectangles of coloured paper

Give everyone a pencil and a rectangle of coloured paper. Ask them to fold the top corners back so that it makes a traditional house shape. Say that this represents the place in which they live (even if it does not look much like it!). On the roof of the house they should write their name. On the main part of the house, they should draw themselves and the people they share their home with. This can include any people who visit their home, so that people who live alone are not excluded. They can go on to add details, such as their pets, furniture, favourite possessions and so on.

Invite everyone to show their 'house' to the person sitting next to them, explaining what the drawings are. They can share what it is about their home that they want to thank God for.

While some music is played or songs are sung, the papers should be collected up and brought to the front. Conclude with a prayer of thanks for all the families that the houses represent. It may be possible after the service to display them on a wall which can remain on show for a few weeks. People who are not present at this service could then add their own homes as a way of thanking God.

(This activity could be extended to an event in a Parents and Toddlers group, where all families could create the symbol of their home, thanking God for it and asking him to bless them. Alternatively, children could expand on the idea in their groups in the following weeks.)

You might also want to include prayers for your local community and for the world, where there are those who are orphaned and homeless.

Prayers of confession

Everyone should join in the response: **Forgive us and help us, we pray.**

Holy God, we confess to you the times when we have failed to treat those in our families with the care you expect of us.

For the things we say which hurt each other,
forgive us and help us, we pray.

For the times when we insist on getting our own way, despite what others feel,
forgive us and help us, we pray.

For times when we increase the tension instead of seeking to make peace,
forgive us and help us, we pray.

For our anger, our lack of respect and our failure to listen,
forgive us and help us, we pray.

And because sometimes we just get bored with each other,
forgive us and help us, we pray.

Amen

Ending the service

Bring the service to a close with the following prayer, which could be read by the leader, with a response. It is also available as a download from **web ref AASA3.Moth_1.**

Lord God, may our families be places of healing.
Teach us to care for them as you do.

May our families be places of service.
Show us how to be helpful to those we live with.

May our families be places of welcome.
May all who visit our homes sense your love.

May our families be places where Jesus is invited.
For your presence truly gives each family something to celebrate.

Amen

Helpful extras

Music and song ideas
Choose songs and hymns about God's gifts of family relationships. These might include: 'God is our Father' (*SOF* 134); 'Bind us together' (*SOF* 43); 'Jesus put this song into our hearts' (*SOF* 299); 'For the beauty of the earth' (*SOF* 112); 'Today I choose' (*SOF* 2083)

Notes and comments

The **Bible retelling** script needs minimal preparation, but would be most effective if the people involved are at least prepared in advance. This may be something you could ask the youth group to do.

Mothering Sunday can be a difficult time for many people, so be sensitive to your congregation's particular situations. When talking about families and family life, be careful not to make anyone feel excluded, particularly single people or couples who do not have children. Be aware of anyone who has lost a parent or child recently, and perhaps include a special time to pray for them. In addition, the opportunities to offer hospitality and use our homes will vary from individual to individual. Be aware of what is possible in the congregation.

Choose the items which are most suited to your situation, trying to involve all ages in the service, without aiming it exclusively at children. Remember that there may be visitors who don't usually attend church, so make your language accessible and welcoming.

Remember, remember

April

Light series: Joshua
Light readings: Joshua 1:1–18; 2:1–24; 3:1–17; 6:1–27

Aims: to see how Joshua inspired God's people to remember
to explore the importance of making sure we remember what God has done

Readings: Joshua 4:1–24; Luke 22:7–20; 1 Corinthians 11:23–26

Getting started

Light, in April 2010, is looking at the early chapters of Joshua, celebrating God's power at work through Joshua as he brought the people of Israel into the land God had promised to Abraham centuries earlier. It is now over forty years since the Israelites had been freed from Egypt by God.

Forty years earlier, they had stood on the edge of the land, had discovered how good it was but observed the strength of the inhabitants and their cities. Despite all they had seen of God's power at work in the events of the exodus, they could not believe that God could give them victory and take them in to the land. Only two people, Caleb and Joshua, trusted God to fulfil his promise. So Joshua was an ideal choice to be the successor to Moses and the one to lead them into the land.

Light looks at the way Joshua encourages the people, sends in new spies to check the position and leads them all through the swollen River Jordan. This service picks up the story at that point. It looks at the importance for the Israelites of remembering all that God had done and encourages us to find ways of remembering all that God has done in our own lives, as individuals and as communities.

You will need:

- memory game items or PowerPoint download for **Beginning the service** from **web ref AASA3.Apr_1**
- props to support the **Bible reading**
- memorial cards PowerPoint – download **web ref AASA3.Apr_2**
- a prominent monument of stones; pebbles or paper 'stones' and felt-tip pens for the **Prayer activity**
- PowerPoint copies of the **Prayer of confession** – download **web ref AASA3.Apr_3**
- **Statement of faith** – download **web ref AASA3. Apr_4**

Beginning the service

With: either a collection of items that can be placed on a tray and memorised, or a PowerPoint presentation of a number of different items (a downloadable version of this suggestion is available from **web ref AASA3.Apr_1**)

Open the service with a fun activity that introduces the idea of memory. There are two suggestions for doing this.

Prepare a tray or a table top with 15 items on it. Cover it with a tea towel or tablecloth. Invite three or four volunteers of different ages to look at the revealed display for 20 seconds, before covering it up again. In turn, they should then name one of the objects. Anyone unable to correctly name an item misses a turn.

Alternatively, use a PowerPoint presentation in which a series of 15 objects are shown on screen for 3 seconds each. They should then be named by volunteers in a similar way to the first method – or, as a further variation, the congregation could be divided into two or three teams to name one item in turn.

At the end, explain the importance of being able to remember things. Ask the congregation to think of things that it is important to remember, or situations in which it is important to remember. Explain that you will be coming back to this theme.

Bible reading

The story from Joshua 4:1–24 is a dramatic one and worth re-enacting. Be as creative as you wish. Three voices are needed for the reading – narrator, Joshua and the Lord. Depending on the size and nature of the congregation, acting parts can also be allocated to:

- the priests, who will need an 'ark' or 'covenant box' of some sort to carry – a cardboard box with two broom handles might be adequate, unless someone wants to be creative and make cherubim and paint it all gold.
- the men who will take the stones from the bed of the Jordan. You will need some stones. These could either be pebbles (you can buy a bag from garden centres – don't be tempted to go to the beach and collect them; there are laws prohibiting it) or 'stones' cut from paper and coloured with felt-tip pens. These stones also feature in the **Prayer activity**.
- the army
- the rest of the people, which could involve all the remaining mobile members of the congregation

Create a 'river' using ribbons, tablecloths or dust sheets. The effect will be more powerful if these can be rolled up to allow safe passage and then released again when everyone has passed over. As the chapter is read, the various groups act out their roles. Ensure that the 'camp' (v 3) is somewhere prominent, as the 'monument' will be used again during the service.

Bible retelling

As actors you will need an elderly man surrounded by a group of children, with his wife in the background, perhaps doing some household task. This provides a good opportunity for children to get involved. It also enables the background from Chapter 3 to be presented, if this is appropriate. This should not be used as an alternative to the reading of Joshua 4 but as a supplement.

One of the children: Grandad, tell us the story of the stones again, pleeease.
Man: Ohhh, that was an amazing day, that was! All those years we had in the desert, and there we were right at the edge of the land that God was going to give us. We could have gone in years earlier – I wasn't alive then – but those who were alive then just didn't believe God could do it. Anyway, there we were, all ready to go, but there in front of us is the great River Jordan, in flood. Twenty metres or more of fast-flowing water, deep too. Some people were afraid: perhaps we wouldn't make it after all.
Wife: As I recall that's what you said.
Man: Anyway, Joshua called the priests with the covenant box. He got them to walk straight into the river – madness, we all thought, certain death. But they weren't washed away. Suddenly, the water stopped flowing and there was dry land. Just like the Red Sea at the exodus, we reckoned. We weren't too sure…
Wife: You certainly weren't…
Man: … but we started to move across – a bit wet underfoot but we all got over safely. Some of the men picked up some big rocks – that's them over there now. They also built a pile in the middle of the river. Then the priests came up out of the river and no sooner were they out than the water came rushing back. That's why those stones are there: to remind us of all that God did, and to stop us forgetting his amazing power and how great he is.

Bible talk

With: cards depicting various 'memorials' or a PowerPoint presentation with headings and replicas of the memorial cards (a general version of this with eight images is available from **web**

ref AASA3.Apr_2); up to three people primed to tell personal and church or community stories, and two people to talk about recent celebratory events

This talk is in three sections, each designed to explore different ways in which we keep memories alive. Explain that we have various ways of keeping memories alive and that three important ones can be found in today's Bible readings.

Memorials or monuments

These can take various forms. Prior to the service, hide cards around the church depicting various memorials. These could reflect local interest and could include a local war memorial or one from the church, a blue plaque from a local house, a gravestone, a photo of a celebration event, a diary or journal, and a statue of a local dignitary. Ask the children to find these and bring them to the front. As they do so, talk about what the children have found and what it might mean, drawing out the significance. Alternatively (or in addition) you could have these on a PowerPoint presentation – this is particularly useful in a large building. Talk about the stones that the Israelites used to build the monument to remind them of God's power. Explain that this was so that they would never forget. We may not build monuments but we can keep special things that remind us of times when God has done special things in our lives. You could invite suggestions as to what these might be.

Telling the story

Read verses 21–24 and explain how important it is to tell our stories. In our families, we tell the stories of significant events and people so that we don't forget. Invite the people who have been primed in advance to tell their stories of events that have been significant. It would be good for one of these to be a personal story and at least one to be a story of something in the life of the church or the community. It's best that these people reflect the diversity of the congregation, including different ages.

Events

Invite two people to be interviewed about recent events – maybe a child has had a birthday and you could talk about what they did, or a couple have celebrated a significant wedding anniversary, or there has been something in the church or local community. Explain that Israel had several festivals every year which helped them to remember what God had done. Christians too have events which help us to remember, such as Christmas or Pentecost. Jesus asked his disciples to remember him in a special meal which has become known

as Holy Communion in our churches. This especially helps us to remember his death and resurrection – if Easter is fresh in the minds of the congregation, make some link here.

Close by reminding everyone how important it is that we never forget what God has done for us. How can we help ourselves to remember?

Prayer activity

With: either pebbles or 'stones' cut from paper (see **Bible reading** above); felt-tip pens

Give everyone two pebbles or stones. Alternatively, people can come to pick a stone from the monument built during the **Bible reading**. Invite them to write on the stones any things for which they are grateful to God. They should write the same thing on each. If there are very young children present, use paper so that while others write, they can draw. Ask everyone to bring one of their stones forward and either build a pile or stick them on a board the shape of a cairn. (They are to keep the other one to take home to help them remember.) Select some of the written items and weave them into a prayer of thanksgiving in which you can lead the congregation. You may want to encourage others to lead this prayer.

Prayers of confession

Everyone should join in the responses. This prayer is available as a download from **web ref AASA3. Apr_3**.

Father God, we are sorry for the times we forget.
Please forgive us and help us to remember.
We are sorry when we forget all the good things that you have done for us.
Please forgive us and help us to remember to honour you.
We are sorry when we forget to thank others.
Please forgive us and help us to remember to be thankful.
We are sorry when we forget to be kind.
Please forgive us and help us to remember to show we care.
We are sorry when we forget to do what you want us to do.
Please forgive us and help us to remember to be obedient.
Father God we are sorry for the times we forget that you are with us.
Please forgive us and help us to remember that you are always there.

Ending the service

With: either pebbles or 'stones' cut from paper; felt-tip pens

Remind people that they have placed one stone on the church 'monument'. Explain that the second one is for them to take home. Suggest they put it somewhere to remind them of what God has done.

Lead them in a prayer of your own or use the following.

Lord God, thank you for all that you have done for us. Help us always to remember and be thankful. As we take these reminders home, please use them to keep our thoughts on you. Amen

Helpful extras

> ## Music and song ideas
> 'Great is thy faithfulness' (*SOF* 147); 'O God, our help in ages past' (*SOF* 415); 'Faithful One' (*SOF* 89); 'The steadfast love of the Lord' (*SOF* 549); 'Be bold, be strong' (*SOF* 37); 'How great is our God' (*SOF* 2065); 'My God is so big' (*ks* 255); 'Our God is an awesome God' (*SOF* 453); 'Today I choose' (*SOF* 2083); 'I am with you' (*Bitesize Bible Songs* CD); 'For ever' (*Bitesize Bible Songs 2* CD)

Statement of faith
This could be said together, responsively, with a leader or with two sides of the congregation taking alternate lines. It is available as a download from **web ref AASA3.Apr_4.** Each statement is in a different colour which splits this statement into four parts with a final sentence.

We remember that you are the God who created the world,
who loves all people,
who sent Jesus into the world to show that love and to die for us.

We remember that Jesus rose from the dead to give us new life.

We remember that you sent your Spirit into the world
and that he is with us now.
We remember that you have given us friends and family in this church.

All this we remember and we are glad.

Notes and comments

Ideally, this service could include Holy Communion or be linked to a Communion service; this could be a very powerful statement of remembering. How you do this will depend on your tradition, and the role that you are happy for children to take in Communion. If you do this, adapt the **Bible talk** as necessary.

You could do something more informal with people sharing bread and wine in small groups. This would capture more of the idea of Passover and the way the early church remembered Jesus as part of a normal meal. It might also make it easier to involve children if this is not part of your normal practice. As Passover was a time for telling the story, it would be possible to split the talk and make the second point (Telling the story) part of the Communion celebration. This would be especially appropriate if someone wants to share their story of coming to faith in Jesus.

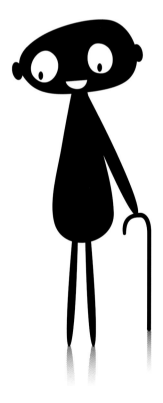

So, who is Jesus?

May or adapt for Pentecost

Light **series:** Only Jesus
Light **readings:** John 14:1–14; 14:15–31; 15:1–17; 16:5–15

Aims: to explore who people thought Jesus was, before his death and at his ascension
to discuss how we understand who Jesus is today

Readings: John 6:1–15; Acts 1:1–11; optional reading, Exodus 16:13–18

Getting started:

This month, the *Light* series has been looking at different 'I am' sayings of Jesus (see the references above). The focus of this all-age service is on another of the sayings, 'I am the bread that gives life' (John 6:35, CEV). We're going to look at the miracle of the feeding of the 5,000 in John 6:5–15. After this miracle, the crowd wanted to crown Jesus as their king. They did not know who he was. Jesus withdrew to the mountains to pray but later, as Jesus was compared with Moses (whom God used to feed his people in the wilderness), he told them that he was himself the Bread of life.

The reading from Acts 1:1–11 reminds us that even after Jesus' resurrection, his disciples did not fully understand who he was and significantly, just before his ascension, asked if he was going to restore a king to Israel. He did not answer but talked about his Father and the role of the Holy Spirit. And then he ascended into the skies!

As Christians living after Pentecost, we have a clearer understanding of who Jesus is but we still have questions and an inadequate understanding. But we experience the Spirit, giving us power to tell others the good news about him, as Jesus promised his disciples. By weaving the John 6 and Acts 1 readings together, you can help people to discover more about Jesus and can look at what the festivals of Ascension Day and Pentecost mean for us today.

You will need:

- a flip chart for **Beginning the service**
- congregational parts of John 6:1–15 for the **Bible reading** on display – download **web ref AASA3.May_1**
- a dramatic version of Acts 1:1–11 for the **Bible reading** – download **web ref AASA3.May_2**
- fish-shape cards for the **Prayer activity**
- bread-shape cards for **Ending the service**
- ingredients to make tuna sandwiches for the **Game** (which is not really an optional extra!) and the **Bible talk**
- prayer for **Ending the service** – download **web ref AASA3.May_3**
- **Statement of faith** – download **web ref AASA3.May_4**

Beginning the service

With: a flip chart to enable you to record people's suggestions; pens

Ask people to help you make a list of the different things they might take on a picnic. Make sure that you get responses from people of different ages to show that everyone has a part to play.

Tell the congregation that today's service is looking at the rather extraordinary picnic Jesus had with a huge number of people. This picnic was important to help Jesus' special friends, the disciples, to realise who Jesus really was. It helps us to think about who Jesus is, too.

Bible reading

Read John 6:1–15 as a drama script. There is a downloadable CEV version from **web ref AASA3.May_1**, which involves the whole congregation. You will need to select three people to read the individual parts (either in advance or on the day). The congregational parts should be projected or printed for everyone. Introduce the different characters.

The reading of Acts 1:1–11 needs someone to play the parts of Luke, Jesus and the two men dressed in white clothes. The part of the apostles can be played by everyone. A downloadable CEV version is available from **web ref AASA3.May_2**. Explain that Luke travelled with the apostle Paul and wrote not only the first part of his account as Luke's Gospel, but also the second part, which we know as the Acts of the Apostles. In this story, it is clear that the disciples are still trying to work out who Jesus is. Do they think he is going to be a king?

Bible talk

With: the five tuna fish sandwiches made earlier in the **Game** (if you did it), or create some to use in this talk

So much food for everyone!
Give out the sandwiches to the groups who cheered the sandwich-makers in the **Game**. Ask each group to keep passing their sandwich round, breaking off a little piece to eat each time it comes round, and to keep going until it has all gone. (Before you pass the sandwiches out, make sure people know exactly what is in them, for the sake of those with relevant allergies, and try to be as hygienic as possible.)

Each group counts how many times the sandwich comes round. If you know roughly how many people are in each group, someone good at mental arithmetic can do a rough calculation of how many little pieces of sandwich there were in total, across the whole congregation. Draw attention to how many there are in church and how hungry you would be if those little nibbles of tuna sandwich were all you had to eat for the day.

Who is Jesus? Not an earthly king
Summarise the story of the feeding of the 5,000 from John 6, emphasising that the disciples had even less food on that day than you've had between you with the tuna sandwiches. Point out how few the tuna sandwiches fed and how hungry you would be when the sandwiches ran out, if that was all you had to eat today.

Remind people that Jesus gave thanks for the five small loaves and two small fish, which were then passed round. More than five thousand people had so much that there was enough to fill 12 baskets with leftovers.

The people were so excited that they wanted to make Jesus their king. They didn't know who he really was. Comment that just before Jesus went back to heaven, even his disciples talked about him restoring an earthly kingdom. Even they still did not know who he really was!

Who is Jesus? The Bread of life
But Jesus was far more than just an earthly king. In John 6:35, after feeding the 5,000, he says 'I am the bread that gives life! No one who comes to me will ever be hungry' (CEV). This is another of the 'I am' sayings, which tell us more about Jesus. Refer to these sayings to reinforce the *Light* theme, and ask for other sayings that the *Light* groups have explored.

Choose the best way to conclude this **Bible talk** according to your knowledge of the congregation and the context of the service. Whatever you decide, remember to keep it brief and simple.

- Either: expand the link with the 'I am' sayings when Jesus says, 'I am the bread that gives life' (John 6:35). In John 6:32, Jesus tells the crowd that his Father gives the true bread from heaven, and that he is himself the bread that gives life to the world: in effect claiming to be God, come from heaven. You could expand on the story of how Moses was used to feed the people in Exodus 16:14,15 to put John 6 in its context. Jesus, the Bread of life, was far more than who Moses was. Jesus gives life to the world. Comment briefly on what that means for us.

- Or: think about how Jesus' ascension emphasises his special mission and identity. Comment on what he said about his own suffering and death, and also his Father and the Holy Spirit. At this stage, he was saying more about them than about himself. Look at what he claimed would happen to his disciples and then how he left them.

He had to leave in order that the Spirit could come in his place, sent from the Father, to be with his followers for ever and to give them power to share the good news. He was not going to be their king nor give them an earthly king. If this service is at Pentecost, pick up especially on what Jesus tells the disciples about waiting in Jerusalem for God to give them the Holy Spirit. God kept his promise, as we know!

Ask someone to give a very short testimony, either of how they discovered more about who Jesus is or of a time when God provided for them in extraordinary ways. In advance, think of a couple of short questions as in an interview and rehearse the answers. Avoid using Christian jargon which might be meaningless to those who aren't regular church attendees, and avoid language that will not communicate with younger people.

Prayer activity

With: small fish shapes about 10 cm long, cut out of grey or silver card (enough for everyone to have one); pencils or pens

Ask people to write on their fish card either a 'thank you' to God for the way he has provided for them in some way, or a prayer asking God to meet a need they have, or a prayer for someone else in need: perhaps a friend or relative who is ill, or someone in the world who does not have enough to eat. Adults will need to help younger children. Children might prefer to express their prayers as pictures.

End the prayer time in one of two ways:

- Either: ask everyone to stand up and hold up their fish. People could take their prayer home, instead of a bread card with John 6:35 written on it (see **Ending the service**). Acknowledge everyone's prayers using this response:

   Leader: Lord Jesus, thank you for coming as the bread from heaven to meet all our needs.
   All: Lord, we bring you our praise, our thanks and our prayers. Amen.

- Or: sing a song or hymn during which all the prayers are collected together into a basket

and brought to the service leader as an offering to God. When the service leader is holding the basket, use the response above.

Ending the service

With: another set of cards in the shape of a bread roll (brown, orange or cream), this time with John 6:35 written on it, that people can take away to read during the week

Remind the congregation that you have heard how people, including Jesus' disciples, had got it wrong and thought Jesus would be a king to rescue them. You have also heard about the amazing picnic that Jesus had provided. He had come to give life to the world. He stills gives life today; he is the bread that gives life.

Remind people to look forward to celebrating Pentecost, when God gave his Holy Spirit to the disciples so that they would have power to tell others about Jesus.

Give out the bread roll cards and say John 6:35 together. It could be a *Learn and remember* verse that you want to come back to at a later service.

Use the following prayer to say together. It is also available as a download from **AASA3. May_3**.

Lord Jesus, thank you for coming as the Bread of life, for us.
Thank you for providing all that we need.
We worship you today and every day.
Please fill us with your Holy Spirit
and help us to tell others about you.
Amen

Helpful extras

Music and song ideas
'Break thou the bread of life' (*SOF* 50); 'I am the bread of life' (*SOF* 200); 'You are the King of Glory' (*SOF* 627); '5000 + hungry folk' (*SOF* 719); 'Thank you, Jesus' (*ks* 313); 'Thank you very much!' (*ks* 314); 'Who spoke words of wisdom and life?' (*ks* 387). If this is Pentecost, you will want to include songs related to the coming of the Spirit such as 'Come down, oh love divine' (*MP* 89); 'Spirit of holiness' (*MP* 611); 'Wind, wind, blow on me' (*MP* 771)

Game

With: space on tables for people to work on and five sets of everything as follows: two slices of bread; a small bowl containing enough butter or margarine to spread on the bread; a small bowl containing enough tinned tuna fish mixed with mayonnaise to go on the bread; a knife for spreading; an unbreakable plate (cardboard, polystyrene); a serviette; plus a bowl of water and a towel to wash hands

Ask for five volunteers to come to the front. Use a mixture of ages, but they all need to be able to make the sandwich. If children volunteer, check with their accompanying adults that it's OK for them to use a knife. If it isn't, ask the accompanying adult to help the child. Each person should make a tuna fish sandwich from the ingredients. Set it up as a race – the winner is the first to make the sandwich, cut it in half, and place it neatly on the plate. Divide the rest of the congregation into five groups, each group cheering their competitor.

Keep the five sandwiches to be used during the **Bible talk**.

Statement of faith:

This is downloadable from **web ref AASA3. May_4**.

Leader: What about you, who do *you* say Jesus is?
Everyone: Jesus is God's anointed Son who died and rose again to bring us forgiveness and new life.
He is our bread that brings us life.
He provides all that we need.
He fills us with his Holy Spirit.
He gives us power to tell others about him.
We give him thanks and praise. Amen

Notes and comments

This service could be used in two contexts, to develop the links with the *Light* series on the 'I am' sayings, or as an ascension or Pentecost service. The reading from John 6 tells the story of Jesus feeding the 5,000, which is then used as a platform to teach about Jesus' identity. He was the Bread of life and greater than Moses. You may wish to include an Old Testament reading from Exodus 16 to give this context.

If this service is used at Pentecost, you will want to place greater emphasis on the ascension, which led on to Pentecost. You will choose the second option to end the **Bible talk**.

If Holy Communion is part of this all-age service, the story of the feeding of the 5,000 from John 6:1–15 makes a very natural link with Jesus as the Bread of life. Jesus' body was broken for us and, just as we share in the broken bread, we share in the bread that gives us life. If this accords with the custom within your church, Communion could be shared in the same groups that ate the tuna sandwich.

Jesus' love goes on and on and…

June

Light **series**: Jesus the healer
Light **readings**: Mark 1:29–39; 1:40–45; 3:1–6; 5:21–43

Aims: to focus on the healing of the woman in the crowd
to recognise Jesus' compassion towards us

Readings: Mark 5:24b–34; Isaiah 41:17–20

Getting started

The readings from this *Light* series have come from the Gospel of Mark, focusing on Jesus the healer and his compassion for those in need around him. The constant theme in these stories is the demands placed on Jesus and the increasing numbers who flocked to him, so much so that in Mark 1:45 we are told he could 'no longer enter a town openly'. This story of the woman who touches Jesus' coat demonstrates both characteristics. The crowd is pressing in on Jesus and he is already on his way to bring Jairus' daughter back from the dead. Yet Jesus finds time to notice and to lovingly address the needs of this woman whose modest hope is that just one touch would heal her. One of the *Light* sessions explores the story of Jairus' daughter.

The woman's ailment is difficult to explain to young children but the **Bible retelling,** without being too explicit, will go some way towards demonstrating the stigma attached and the consequences, such as her inability to have children. It is worth noting that the woman was in a constant state of ceremonial uncleanness, while the daughter, at the age of 12, would be about to enter puberty, when she too would experience regular uncleanness. Jesus shows that such conditions are no barrier to him. What is more, the woman had been suffering for the whole length of the girl's life. Jesus' compassion is vast and breaks all boundaries, which is what you would want every person in the service to grasp hold of.

You will need:

- a picture of the woman in the crowd downloaded from the Internet or from **web ref AASA3.Jun_2** for **Beginning the service** and **Bible talk**
- images for the **Bible reading** from Isaiah 41 downloaded from **web ref AASA3.Jun_1**
- a slide show or collection of pictures of local people with responsibility for people's lives (create your own) for the **Bible talk**
- paper in the shape of a speech bubble or sticky labels, pens and an outdoor coat for the **Prayer activity**

Beginning the service

With: picture of the woman touching Jesus' clothing, for example *Touch of Faith* by Simon Dewey (http://www.christcenteredmall.com/stores/art/dewey/touchoffaith.htm) or the illustrations from *Jesus puts things right* (Scripture Union) from **web ref AASA3.Jun_2**

Ask if anyone can think of a celebrity they would go out of their way to see and get close to if this person came to your town. If they got close enough to touch or speak, what would they do or say? Would they want an autograph, an answer to a burning question, or to have their photo taken with this star? What if they could only touch the celebrity's coat? Would it still be worth the hassle of fighting through the crowds?

Display the picture(s) and ask what is happening here. What could the woman be doing, and why? Explain that you will be hearing the story of a woman who tried very hard to get close to Jesus.

Bible reading

The reading from Isaiah 41:17–20 suits a visual representation of a dry desert covered with flowing water, which leads to the flourishing of plants. This could be done on a screen with pictures stuck on, or on a PowerPoint as a download from **web ref AASA3.Jun_1**, or (with a small group) three-dimensionally in a sandpit with a jug of water and some plants.

Begin with an image of someone in a dry and dusty place.
In verse 18, add water by showing two or three different pictures for rivers, pools and flowing water to drink, when they are mentioned.
In verse 19, add several plants or trees, as they are mentioned, with a general impression of well-watered land and people. The finished picture should look lush and green in comparison with the start.

The reading of Mark 5:24b–34 could be read slowly with four well-rehearsed freeze-frames as follows: actors freeze as a crowd presses around Jesus (vs 24b); the woman reaches out to touch Jesus' cloak (vs 27–29); Jesus turns to notice the woman as his disciples look on, astonished (vs 30–32); Jesus holds the woman by the hand, or places his hands on her head (vs 33,34), while she smiles.

Bible retelling

This retelling could be read or spoken from memory by three noticeably different voices: a resigned husband, a scandalised disciple and a woman full of awe. Each one picks up the last speaker's story where they left off. Introduce the three characters.

Husband: That day started like any other. I went off to work and left her in her room, calling out 'goodbye' through the door. We lived and slept separately, of course – had done for the last 12 years. Being any closer to her would have made me unclean, just like her. She, of course, was not allowed anywhere near the Jewish meeting place. It's hardly what we expected when we got married, but life just turns out like that sometimes, doesn't it? I'd got over the sadness of not being able to be close to her. We'd worked out how to express our love for each other in words instead of touch. Not being able to have children was harder to bear. But after 12 years, I wasn't expecting any changes. It was just a normal morning.

Disciple: We were trying to hurry Jesus to get to the important official's daughter. His name was Jairus – of course, I don't know the girl's name, but from the sound of it, she was pretty sick. The crowds didn't understand the urgency. We were having to do the bodyguard thing again – pushing our way through, trying to ignore all the shouting and crying as people swarmed out of the houses, bringing sick people, disabled people, disturbed people and sad people to Jesus, dozens and dozens of them. It was like a scrum.

Then, out of the blue, Jesus stopped dead in his tracks and asked, 'Who touched me?' I mean, honestly! What a daft question! I told him; I said, 'Lord, in case you hadn't noticed, there's a whole crowd of people here, jostling you and bumping you from every side. They've all touched you!' But he insisted. He said that he'd felt power go out of him.

I was about to force him to move on again when a woman was half pushed, and half fell forward from the crowd and landed at his feet. Her face was bright red and she was stammering something; she looked scared stiff and was shaking all over. Jesus leaned forward to hear what she was saying. I only caught a few words – 'bleeding' and '12 years' and 'doctors'. Enough to realise what she'd just done. She'd gone and made him ritually unclean – right when he was on his way to an important synagogue ruler's house! You see, people who are reckoned to be unclean and not allowed into worship can make someone else unclean just by touching them.

Woman: But Jesus wasn't angry. In fact, he looked at me ever so kindly and helped me to my feet.

He said, 'Your faith has healed you. Go in peace.' And I felt suddenly full of peace and joy, and I knew that this would last – that everything was going to be different now. I couldn't wait to get home and tell my husband. The first thing I did was move all my things out of that little room where I'd lived for the past 12 years. That room's a nursery now.

Bible talk

With: a slide show/pictures of people known to the congregation who may have responsibility for people's lives

Talk about important people who have some responsibility in our lives such as teachers, police, and politicians. How can we approach them – in person, by phone, email, letter? They are often very busy and hidden by mounds of bureaucracy. Go through the pictures (and adapt to your situation) and ask what the basic rules for approaching these people are.

– **Your teacher:** you have to put your hand up! (The average 4-year-old asks about four hundred questions a day. Even if they only asked half of those questions at school, in a class with 30 children a teacher might be faced with 6,000 questions a day!)
– **The head teacher:** you might need to go to their office, or make an appointment.
– **A policeman:** you need to dial 999 or go to the police station – if it is open!
– **Your local MP:** you have to write a letter or an email or phone
– **The Queen:** there are plenty of rules for meeting the Queen, including addressing her as 'Your Majesty' first and thereafter, 'Ma'am'; not speaking until spoken to; never leaving a room before she does (or if you do, walking out backwards!)

We have rules about approaching such people, and often it is a scary thing to do. The woman in this story must have seen Jesus as a very important person and, moreover, the only hope she had left. But he was on his way to the house of a very important person and she did not want to make too much of a demand on his time. So she chose to just touch his coat, knowing that it would be enough to heal her. Perhaps she did not feel she deserved anything more. Show the images from **web ref AASA3.Jun_2**.

Jesus, however, insisted on knowing who it was he had just healed. He wanted to show the woman that he was approachable, and that he had time for her, too. He wanted her to grow in her faith. She was just as special and important to him as the man whose daughter he was on his way to

heal. Jesus' care for this woman was generous and overflowing. Refer back to the reading from Isaiah 41, where God's generosity and care is overflowing, rich and abundant. This is what Jesus was like.

Explain that we too can approach Jesus, no matter how small we feel. His love is never-ending. What is more, there are no rules about approaching him – you don't have to put your hand up, make an appointment or use a particular name or language to address him. Instead, he loves us and wants to listen to us.

Finish by saying that Jesus changed the rules about the approachability of God. Once, only certain people could approach God directly, in certain places and at certain times, only using certain words or after sacrifices had been made. But Jesus says that everyone can come to the Father through him. (Open your arms out wide in welcome.) Jesus welcomed this unwanted sick but trusting woman. He welcomes us with his love that never ends.

Prayer activity

With: paper in the shape of a speech bubble (enough for everyone), or sticky labels; pens; an outdoor coat or ceremonial garment such as a surplice

Lay the garment out on the floor or hang it up on a coat stand. Explain that the woman who touched Jesus' clothing knew that just one touch could be enough to answer her prayer, but Jesus wanted to give her much more than healing. He wanted to see her, speak with her and listen to her story. Today we can approach Jesus and be close to him. Encourage people to spend time with Jesus, being quiet and listening to his voice.

First encourage everyone to close their eyes and imagine that they are in the crowd jostling to get close to Jesus. How irritated are they when someone gets in the way or when it looks as though they are not going to get a good look at Jesus' face?

Now ask them to imagine that Jesus has stopped and the people in front of them have fallen back so that they are standing in full view of Jesus, but he is moving on. But then he stops and turns towards them. They look into his eyes. What do they feel? Embarrassed, surprised, overwhelmed, joyful? What do they want to say to him?

Play the Iona song 'A touching place' in the background and encourage people to write or draw what they want to say to Jesus on their speech bubble/sticky label. Invite people to place their bubble on the garment or stick it onto the coat that is hanging up.

Prayers of confession

The confession could be introduced with reference to the woman's situation. She felt unclean and unworthy, ashamed to approach Jesus directly; perhaps she even worried that her illness would have a bad effect on him (by making him ritually unclean). In the same way, our sin and guilt makes it difficult to approach God. We may even imagine that we are just too bad for him to want to relate to us. However, God accepts and forgives us, whatever we have done.

In the story, the woman is scared but she 'tells the whole truth' to Jesus. Allow some quiet time for people to do the same. This could be followed by liturgical words of confession and absolution, or by speaking the words from the reading: 'Your faith has healed you. Go in peace.'

Ending the service

With: the picture from **Beginning the service**

Look back at the picture of the woman touching Jesus' coat and ask people to think about where they would place themselves in the picture – are they a disciple, confident in how close they are to Jesus? Or are they the woman, feeling unworthy in his presence but having faith in his power? Or are they Jairus, badly needing Jesus' help and wishing he'd hurry up? Or are they a member of the crowd who is seeing Jesus in action for the first time?

Encourage the congregation that all the people in the picture must have gone away from that situation changed by their experience of Jesus' care and concern for the woman.

Hold your arms out wide in welcome and acceptance and say the following:

Jesus' words are true for us too: Your faith has healed you. Go in peace.
We thank you, Lord Jesus, that you have broken down the barriers that separate us from God.
We are so grateful that you welcome us with arms wide open.
We rejoice that your love goes on and on and on. Amen and amen!

Helpful extras

Music and song ideas
'Love divine, all loves excelling' (*SOF* 377);
'My song is love unknown' (*SOF* 400);
'The steadfast love of the Lord' (*MP* 666);
'Peace is flowing like a river' (*SOF* 458);
'My God is so big' (*ks* 255); 'Jesus' love is very wonderful' (*ks* 208); 'Be kind and compassionate' (John Hardwick *Action Packed {Praise 2 CD*)

For the **Prayer activity** 'A touching place' ('Iona' from *God never sleeps* CD, by John Bell)

Notes and comments

The reading and the theme for the service opens up the possibility for an extended time of prayer for healing in whichever form suits the congregation, perhaps with laying on of hands or anointing with oil. The **Prayer activity** could be merged with this or could lead into it. Alternatively, prayers for healing could be offered after the main service.

Emphasising Jesus' compassion for us as we approach him would be a good way to introduce an invitation to Communion. You may also wish to refer back to the end of the **Bible talk** and further develop the idea of being able to approach God through Jesus.

Take that!

July

***Light* series:** Judges rule God's people
***Light* readings:** Judges 4:1−24; 6:11−16,33−40; 7:1−22; 13:1−7; 16:4−31

Aims: to hear the story of Judge Ehud, the left-hander
to see how God sometimes uses unexpected means to protect or provide for his people

Readings: Judges 3:12−30; Luke 5:1−11

Getting started

Light users have been engaging with the stories in the book of Judges, stories that are not often told in full to children and young people. There is an air of déjà vu about this book. From Othniel (Judges 3) to Samson (Judges 13−16) there are more than two hundred years of Israel's history. People are committed to God's ways and all is going well. Then they lose their focus, do their own thing and life goes horribly wrong. At these times, God called someone (the 'Judge') to rescue the nation and bring them back to the promise they made to Joshua on his death bed. There, they declared, 'We really choose God' (Joshua 24:24). Sadly too often, too quickly, this became, 'We rarely choose God.' The results were disastrous.

Sex, violence, rape, massacre, incest, brutality and deceit litter the book of Judges. But don't shy away from the mess and the gore. We do Scripture a great disservice if we varnish it with a veneer of 'niceness'. The story of Ehud, in this service, is one of the lesser known stories. It is gory, but it has an appeal since it is about a left-hander, about the triumph of the good, about God's appointed man who took the initiative. It has a genuine appeal for boys! This will be a different and maybe challenging all-age service to run, but it will be worth accepting the challenge. At the same time, don't let the horror obscure key points that Judges reveals:
- in all the mess, God remembers his people
- God uses the unlikely ones (like you and me) to work out his purpose
- people's continual disobedience highlights the need for a saviour

You will need:

- a PowerPoint of famous left-handed people from **web ref AASA3.Jul_1** or other left-handed details for **Beginning the service**
- illustrations of Ehud to use in the **Bible retelling** – download **web ref AASA3.Jul_2**
- character cards for the **Bible talk** and additional information – download **web ref AASA3. Jul_3**
- sheets of coloured paper, felt-tip pens and/or paint in trays, scissors, a large roll of paper, bowls of water and towels for the **Prayer activity**
- pictures of church members who work in the community for **Prayers of intercession**

Beginning the service

With: a PowerPoint showing pictures of famous left-handed people (this can be downloaded from **web ref AASA3.Jul_1**) or their names on an OHP acetate (If neither is available, print the names on A3 paper and ask members of the congregation to hold them up. You can find thousands of names on www.anythingleft-handed.co.uk and images can be found using an Internet search engine.)

If you can't access this, here are some suggestions:

Pierce Brosnan   Michael Crawford
Robert de Niro   Marilyn Monroe
Oprah Winfrey   Bill Bryson
Germaine Greer   Bart Simpson
Paul McCartney   Paul Daniels
Damon Albarn   Mozart

Ask if people know what all these people have in common. Give clues if people are struggling to answer.

When the answer is revealed, ask any left-handed members of the congregation to reveal themselves. Find out if any struggled with anything as a result of being left-handed. (Some may be old enough to have gone to schools where using the left hand was discouraged; some may use their cutlery the 'wrong' way round; some may claim that their left-handedness has contributed to their creativeness or has helped them bat for England!) Point out that being left-handed is considered strange: the Latin for 'left-handed' is 'sinister'; the French for 'left' is *gauche* which is not a complimentary term. Books on left-handedness are shelved amongst the 'special needs' section of the library. How affirming is that?

Introduce today's story by saying it is about how God used a 'lefty' to defeat Israel's oppressor. God can use all sorts of people!

Sing a song that praises God for the way he works (see **Music and song ideas**).

Bible reading

The reading from Luke 5:1–11 is a New Testament example of how Jesus used an ordinary fisherman who was going about his business and didn't feel up to the job of serving the Lord. This could be read as a script with a narrator, Jesus and Peter.

Bible retelling

Use this 'poem' to retell Ehud's story. The effect will be more dramatic if a church member is able to commit this to memory and can perform it rather than read it. An artistic member of the church might be able to illustrate the story in advance, projecting the drawings. Seven cartoons are available from **web ref AASA3.Jul_2**. These cartoons by Ian Potter are taken from *A tent peg, a jawbone and a sheepskin rug* (SU) written by Malc Halliday, who wrote this service outline. They are used with his permission. Show the images as indicated, as the poem is read.

Alternatively, ask some of the children to act out the poem as it is being read.

After 40 years of peace
The people turned away.
They thought they'd take control,
That God had had his day. *(Image 1 and pause)*

King Eglon saw his chance,
To Israel he would go
Overwhelm the land
And settle in Jericho.

He ruled for 18 years
Till the people all cried out,
'O save us, Lord our God,'
Was the nature of their shout.

God listened to their cry,
He acted for their good.
He sent his right-hand man,
A lefty, named Ehud.

Ehud wore a great, long coat
With his sword strapped on below.
Set off to see the king
Just – he said – to say hello.

He brought the king a gift *(Image 2)*
What it was we are not told
But I'm guessing it was food,
Hot, roasted, grilled or cold.

The reason for my guess
Is, Eglon was quite a size, *(Image 3)*
If you saw him for yourself
You would know who ate the pies.

Ehud gave the king his gift
Saying, 'I have something to share.' *(Image 4)*
So the king dismissed his guards,
Leaving just the two men there.

'The message is from God,'
Said Ehud with a grin,

Then he whipped out his sword
And quickly stabbed it in.

Into the king's grand robe – *(Image 5)*
Into his flabby skin –
Through fat, muscles and all his guts –
Then further, further in.

The king was quite surprised,
It wasn't what he planned,
Killed by an Israelite
With a sword in his left hand.

The sword kept sinking faster.
The king sank faster still.
Ehud made his escape
Over the windowsill.

The servants found the door locked. *(Image 6)*
They did not know what to do.
They didn't want to burst in,
(the king might be on the loo).

Eventually they entered. *(Image 7)*
Eglon alas – no more,
But lots of his remains
Were spread out on the floor.

Ehud called his people,
Telling Israel to hurry,
'Eglon the king is dead.
There's an end to all our worry.'

Eglon's army was defeated,
And when the fighting ceased
Ehud became their leader
And brought 80 years of peaced (er… peace).

Bible talk

With: cards printed as below and placed in
advance around the meeting space on walls, pillars,
under chairs or pews, on the lectern… wherever
they can still be reached by small hands – a card
should either have the name or the description

GIDEON
I HID FROM GOD'S MESSENGER

MOSES
I AM NOT A GOOD SPEAKER

JEREMIAH
I AM TOO YOUNG

RAHAB
I WAS A PROSTITUTE IN JERICHO

SAUL
I WAS THE ENEMY OF THE CHURCH

PETER
I DIDN'T FEEL GOOD ENOUGH TO SERVE
JESUS

BOY IN THE CROWD
I JUST HAD A FEW LOAVES AND FISH

CORRIE TEN BOOM
I WAS A MIDDLE-AGED WOMAN WHEN
THE ENEMY ARMY ENTERED MY LAND

JONI EARECKSON TADA
I WAS PARALYSED FROM THE NECK DOWN
WHEN I WAS 17

Ask the children to find the cards and match them
up. Talk through the stories of these people and
how God used them even though they seemed
unlikely candidates. If you are not sure who these
people are (and what they did), download **web
ref AASA3.Jul_3**.

How were they able to be useful? Talk of people
who learned to trust God even when they were
not sure of the outcome. If there are members
of the congregation who have good stories to
tell about how God has used them, ask them in
advance if they would be prepared to tell that
story. There may be others in the service whom
you have not thought of, or you may not be aware
of their story, so give an invitation for others
to contribute, but insist that storytelling is brief.
The website www.thereprobablyis.com contains
thousands of stories of 'ordinary people' and why
they believe in God. There may be stories there
that you want to tell at this point.

Draw the thoughts back to the story of Ehud and
the fisherman, Peter. Check that everyone has
grasped what Ehud did. Highlight the fact that as a
left-hander, Ehud would not have been respected
in his society; however, the fact that his sword was
on the less common right side was the reason
he got in to see the king without his sword being
detected. Acknowledge that Peter the fisherman
was only an ordinary man and did not feel good
enough to serve Jesus. But God used them
both – to rescue a nation and to be one of the
founding members of the early Church.

Ask people to consider what God might be asking
them to do this week, and for faith to believe that
he can give them the strength to do this.

Prayer activity

With: sheets of coloured paper; felt-tip pens;
scissors; and/or paint in trays around the building;
a large roll of paper firmly in place at the front of
the meeting space; bowls of water and towels to

wash hands

Ask people to look at their hands. What will they do with them this week? How might their hands be used to encourage, to help, and to do the things that please God? How might their hands be used to hurt, damage and do things that make God sad? After a time of silence, lead people in this prayer:

Lord Jesus, your hands touched the outsider, welcomed and embraced children and healed the sick.
Use our hands this week to do good and not evil.
Use our hands this week to bring blessing and not sadness.
Use our hands this week to build your kingdom and not destroy it. Amen

Ask people to draw round their hand on a sheet of coloured paper, cut it out and place their hand shape at the front of the church meeting space as a sign of their commitment to allow God to use them this week.

Or, if you are using the paint, ask people to place a hand in the paint tray and make a handprint on the roll of paper that has been put up for this purpose.

Prayers of intercession

With: pictures of church members who work in the community on a PowerPoint, or ask these people to be prepared to share something about what they do.

Pray for these people as the pictures are shown or after they have told their stories.

Ending the service

Jesus ascended to heaven and there is an apocryphal story told of an angel who asks him what provision he has made for his work on earth to continue. Jesus says he has left 11 people on earth to do the work. 'And what happens,' asks the angel, 'if they let you down?' Jesus replies, 'There is no other plan.'

Pray the following prayer in a thoughtful way:

It does not matter how strong or confident we do or don't feel.
It does not matter if we use our left or right hand.
It does not matter if we have just a small amount of bread to give.
It does not matter if we are the oldest or the youngest person here today.
God will use us.

We may not know when or how; but if we let him, we will be the people who can change the world for him.

Conclude by singing 'An army of ordinary people'.

Helpful extras

Music and song ideas
'Our God is an awesome God' (*SOF* 453); 'It's amazing' (*SOF* 1902); 'O Lord my God (How great thou art)' (*SOF* 425); 'Your love is amazing' (*SOF* 1676); 'An army of ordinary people' (*SOF* 20); 'Holding nothing back' by Tim Hughes (It is worth looking on www.youtube.com for a downloadable version of this song. It is also on the album entitled *Holding nothing back*.); 'O Jesus, I have promised' (*SOF* 418); 'Take my life' (*SOF* 519 or *SOF* 2037)

Notes and comments

For more information for the **Prayer activity**, 'Loving Hands' in *Multi-sensory Prayer* by Sue Wallace (SU), page 53, underlines that it is our ordinary hands (left or right) that God will use.

In *Multi-sensory Prayer* (see above), activity 29 (page 26) offers a version of the Lord's Prayer that uses hands to express the words of the prayer. If you would normally use the Lord's Prayer in your worship, this might be an appropriate variation.

Although left-handed people are not technically 'special needs', this would be a good time to focus upon those in church who do have special educational needs, whatever they might be. Ask someone in a wheelchair how they cope when they come into the church building – or someone who has a hearing loss or someone who is dyslexic. Then lead a time of prayer, that the church will be welcoming for all. It is worth noting that because of the inclusive nature of all-age worship, you expect more people with special needs to be present, although they might not want to draw attention to this. *Top Tips on Welcoming Special Children* (SU) will give you useful insights.

Lost property

August

Light series: Love stories
Light readings: Luke 10:25–37; 14:15–24; 15:1–7; 15:11–32

Aims: to develop the theme of the 'Lost' stories in Luke
to see how God searches for his people, not wanting anyone to be lost

Readings: Deuteronomy 7:6–11; Luke 15:1,2,8–10

Getting started

During August, *Light* explores the parables in Luke's Gospel in which Jesus helps his hearers explore the depth of God's love for his world and our response to this. The parables of the lost sheep and the prodigal son in Luke 15 each have a *Light* session. Through all these parables runs the message of the value God places on those who are lost – searching for, welcoming and delighting over those who come to him. God's love in these stories is in stark contrast to the exclusiveness of the religious elite of the time who complained that Jesus was mixing with sinners. This affirming message is radically different to religious teachings that emphasise human effort to reach God, rather than God's effort to make himself available to us.

This service can be used at any point during the month, as it addresses themes that are explored in greater depth in *Light*. Attendance during the month of August is usually variable due to holidays and a lack of routine, so this service also stands as a self-contained unit and is not dependent on previous knowledge gained in other *Light* sessions.

You will need:

- lost property stories or facts for **Beginning the service**
- a treasure chest for the **Bible reading**, **Bible talk** and **Ending the service**
- items of lost treasure – a large coin (a large cardboard circle covered in silver foil), a torch, a brush, a phone (old and not valuable) for the **Bible talk**
- chocolate coins for **Ending the service**
- one card for each person (six options with different items of lost property printed on them can be downloaded from **web ref AASA3.Aug_2**) for the **Game** and the **Prayer activity**

Beginning the service

Begin by telling everyone a story about something that you once lost and either eventually found or that, after contacting the appropriate lost property office, you gave up on. If you do not have such a story to tell, ask around the congregation in advance to identify someone who can share their experience. Alternatively, ask someone who works in a school to tell everyone about what might be found in a school's lost property box. They could even bring examples – the more humorous the better! Then, explain that during the service, you will be exploring the theme that God searches for his lost property, his people, because he doesn't want any to be lost.

Here are some lost property facts. (There are many more on the Internet.)

* TfL finds over 156,000 pieces of lost property each year on buses, Tubes, taxis, trains, trams and stations, with even more property lost on other forms of transport in London.
* During the year, Strathclyde Police Force holds public auctions to sell the unclaimed items that are handed in to their lost property office; it is an opportunity for any member of the public to pick up items such as jewellery, cameras, cycles, garden equipment, clothing and electrical goods, with all items going to the highest bidder and no reserve prices set.
* Operation Bike: Sussex Police are listing recovered pedal cycles to try to reunite them with their owners.

Bible reading

With: a large box decorated as a treasure chest with a label 'Treasure' on it

Read Deuteronomy 7:6–11 early in the service to emphasise the message that God values his people. The NIV includes the phrase 'treasured possession'. Explain that God had rescued his people from Egypt through Moses and was reminding them just how precious they were to him. Invite everyone to focus on the treasure chest during the reading.

With a few simple actions, the congregation can participate in the reading of Luke 15:1,2,8–10, as below from the CEV. Introduce the actions before the reading begins, with someone to demonstrate them from the front. The reader should pause to allow time for the actions.
Tax collectors and sinners were all crowding around to listen to Jesus. (*Everyone leans forward cupping an ear with a hand.*)
So the Pharisees and the teachers of the Law of Moses started grumbling, 'This man is friendly with sinners. He even eats with them.'
(*Everyone turns down the corners of their mouth with their fingers.*)
Jesus told the people another story:
What will a woman do if she has ten silver coins and loses one of them? (*Everyone counts to nine on their fingers.*)
Won't she light a lamp, sweep the floor, and look carefully until she finds it? (*Everyone looks under their chair and on the floor.*)
Then she will call in her friends and neighbours and say, 'Let's celebrate! I've found the coin I lost.' (*Everyone does a celebratory dance, similar to one a footballer might do when he has scored a goal.*)
Jesus said, 'In the same way God's angels are happy when even one person turns to him.'

Bible retelling

There are two books which retell the story of the lost coin: *Belcher Bridget* by Alexander Brown in the Crazy Stories Series (SU) and *Jack Black and the Midnight Snack* by Leena Lane (SU). Although targeting the 5 to 8-year-old age range, they will engage the whole congregation if read by a good storyteller. *Belcher Bridget* is available as a download, with illustrations, and as an audio version from **web ref AASA3.Aug_1.** For more details of this fun series of books, see page 87.

Bible talk

With: a treasure chest (see the **Bible reading**); items of lost treasure: a large coin (a large cardboard circle covered in silver foil); a torch; a brush and a phone (use one that is old and not valuable to avoid it being permanently lost)

Before the service, distribute the lost treasure around the building in positions where they won't be accidently moved before the **Bible talk**.

Explain that you are searching for some lost property. Some treasure is missing and you need people's assistance to find it. This treasure will help you understand what Jesus was teaching when he told the story of the lost coin. Ideally, you should go to search for the items, demonstrating the message that God actively seeks for his people.

God cares about anyone who is lost
Ask if anyone has seen a large coin. People may point this out, or someone might have found it. Go and collect the coin. In the story of the lost coin, Jesus says that the woman had ten coins belonging to her, which might have been coins for spending or to decorate her headdress. (Use the word 'belonging' since 'belonging to God' is the opposite of what it means to be 'lost and far

from God'.) Although she still had nine coins, she was concerned that even one of her coins was missing. Jesus wanted his listeners to realise that God cares about people who are lost. Explain that 'lost' means anyone who does not 'belong to God'. People might do bad things, let God down, ignore him and say bad things about him, but he still loves them. In *Light, t*he children will (have) explore(d) this theme further in the parable of the great banquet (Luke 14:15–24) and the other 'Lost' stories. Refer to Deuteronomy 7:6 when Moses reminds the Israelites that they are God's treasured possession. Place the coin in the treasure chest.

God makes a huge effort to find anyone who is lost

Ask for people to look for the torch and the brush, and again go to collect them. This woman put a lot of effort into finding her lost coin, even though she still had another nine others. Make use of the torch and brush to demonstrate the woman's energetic search. Jesus put a lot of effort into searching for people who are lost. He came to this earth to live and die. He showed people what God was like and he searched out and befriended many unpopular sinners. This upset many respectable people. Place the torch and the brush in the treasure chest.

God celebrates when he finds someone who is lost

The final piece of treasure to search for is the phone. Go in search of the treasure and take possession of the phone. Pretend to call someone, and excitedly tell them you found all the treasure! In the story, the woman was so excited about finding the lost coin, that she told her friends. God is also delighted when someone says sorry for the wrong they have done and says that they want to belong to him. He shares his delight with the angels. This theme of God celebrating when the lost return to him is common in all the 'Lost' stories. Place the phone into the treasure chest.

Ask the congregation to cheer because you have found all your lost property.

Remove the items from the chest. Hold up each item and summarise the message it communicates. Put the coin and the phone back into the treasure chest but give the brush and torch to members of the congregation. If God values the lost so much, then surely we need to join in the search for any who do not yet belong to him. Give examples of how people can do this, either on their own or as a church.

Prayer activity

With: the lost property cards (see the **Game**); the treasure chest (see **Bible talk**); a pen or pencil for everyone

If you have not played the 'Lost Property' **Game** or used the treasure chest in an earlier part of the service, distribute one 'lost property' card to everyone and place the treasure chest at the front of the church.

Your aim is to encourage people to pray for one individual who is 'lost property', who does not yet belong to God. Ask everyone to think of someone who needs to know that they are important to God and who doesn't know God very well at the moment. The name of this person should be written on the back of their 'lost property' card. Some people may want to write their own name, or draw a picture. These cards are then placed in the treasure chest. The symbolic gesture of placing a picture of ordinary lost property into the treasure chest expresses a belief that everyone is valuable to God.

Once all the cards are in the treasure chest, lift it up and say the following prayer:

Thank you, Father, that you love these people whose names are in this treasure chest.
Thank you that Jesus came to search for them.
Help us to show them what you are like.
May they recognise that you want them to belong to you.
May they allow you to welcome them.
Amen

Prayer of confession

This prayer recognises that Christians can be complacent. Explain that no matter how long someone has been a Christian, they can let God down and behave as though they do not belong to him. Everyone should join in the emboldened response: **We are sorry and turn back to you now.**

Leader: Father God, sometimes we say things that have let you and other people down.
Everyone: We are sorry and turn back to you now.

Leader: Sometimes we have done things that have let you or other people down.
Everyone: We are sorry and turn back to you now.

Leader: Sometimes we have thought things that have let you and other people down.
Everyone: We are sorry and turn back to you now. Amen

Conclude these prayers of confession with an upbeat celebratory song, to reflect God's pleasure at people repenting.

Ending the service

With: the treasure chest; chocolate coins (available from high street chocolate shops) should already be placed inside

Remind people that you began the service by talking about lost property, and heard how Jesus came searching for his lost property, his people, because God doesn't want anyone to be lost. Open the treasure box, remove the chocolate coins and distribute one coin to everyone in the congregation. This coin should remind people that the coin was searched for and then found. Ask everyone to take their coin home and wait until later in the week to eat it. They could even hide their coins away so they are 'lost' and then eat them together as a family. As they eat, encourage people to thank God that he searches for the 'lost' and to pray for the person they prayed for during the service.

Repeat Deuteronomy 7:6: 'For you are a people holy to the LORD your God … his treasured possession.'

Helpful extras

Game
With: one card for each person (six options with different items of lost property printed on them); volunteers to distribute the cards, which should be well mixed – templates for six different items of lost property are available to download from **web ref AASA3.Aug_2**

This game gives everyone the experience of searching and the delight of finding. Everyone should be given one lost property card. Their task is to find the people with the same lost property item. Ideally, you want there to be approximately twelve people with the same item. The winning group is either the first complete group or the one that has the largest group after three minutes. Draw attention to the effort it took to find people, the delight people felt once they were united and the frustration of the groups that were still incomplete once the game was over.

Notes and comments
Other ways to introduce the theme of 'lost property' at **Beginning the service** could be to try to reunite the contents of your church lost property box with the owners; or the worship leader could announce that they have lost their music book and the whole congregation must look for it before the first song can be sung; or a member of the congregation could interrupt and announce they have lost something important (which is well hidden in the building), and ask several people to help look for it. More could be made of this, if at regular appropriate intervals in the service this person returns to tell you they haven't found it yet. Finally, towards the end of the service, they should announce they *have* found it. Encourage cheering!

This service provides an opportunity to learn about a local community project that aims to express God's value for people on the margins of society, and to show through actions and words what God is like. Projects could include those working with homeless people, drug abusers, refugees, families with needs or some other relevant group. Make sure you use simple and clear language that is accessible to all ages.

We're in this together!

September

Light **series**: Sharing the good news
Light **readings**: Acts 18:1–28; 19:1–12, 23–41; 20:1–16

Aims: to identify as far as possible with Paul's commitment to the Ephesian Christians, aware of what the future held
to explore together what it means to share the gospel with others

Readings: Acts 20:13–38; Exodus 4:18– 21

Getting started

In *Light* throughout September, groups will travel with Paul through the Acts of the Apostles. The purpose of his journeys was to share the good news with whoever would listen. His 'normal' pattern was to start with the Jews and then debate with the Gentiles after many of the Jews often rejected the message. Several times Paul went through Ephesus, including, at one point, staying there for three years. Many people came to faith, although there was active opposition from others. The passage for today's service comes at the end of those journeys as Paul is heading for Jerusalem. He meets with the leaders of the Ephesian church for the last time.

Prophetic words had told Paul that he was facing a time of trial and difficulty, as well as the fact that he would not meet these leaders again. In effect, we have here Paul's summary of what he wants to leave with the church at Ephesus. He reminds them of how he worked: gently and with tears, but not holding back on the hard implications of responding to the good news; never dependent on others, but always serving them, both Jew and Gentile. He now tells the leaders *they* must look after their flock and be dependent on God alone – Paul has discharged the duty to which God called him, with a loving and humble heart.

All-age services are a great opportunity to remind everyone that the body of Christ is made of many parts, each with a role to play – different, but of equal value. In the light of the theme of 'being in it together', today's service should be characterised by great joy *and* hard thinking!

You will need:

- PowerPoint pictures of people or groups and the things or people they care for (these can be downloaded from **web ref AASA3. Sept_1** for the **Bible talk**), A4 sheets with the same pictures jumbled up, pens or pencils
- a large heart on a sheet of card, glue sticks, heart-shaped confetti for the **Prayer activity**
- the **Prayer of confession** can be downloaded from **web ref AASA3.Sept_3**
- the **Statement of faith** can be downloaded from **web ref AASA3.Sept_4**.

Beginning the service

Interview a parent with an older child (13 plus if possible) about their experiences on the first day of school when the child was 4 or 5, and contrast their experiences. If possible, display some photos on the screen of their first day, but without causing embarrassment.

Ask the parent what they told the child and what they told the teacher. Ask the child what they would like to have known and what they were told. Ask the parent how they felt, leaving their child at school all day for the first time. If there are any foundation stage teachers in the congregation, ask them what they would like to have known too. (This may be particularly valuable for any parents with young children.)

This service is about how much the apostle Paul cared for the Christian leaders in the city of Ephesus whom he arranged to meet as he travelled down the Turkish coast on his way to Jerusalem, knowing that he would never see them again. He wanted to prepare them for life without him.

An alternative introduction would be to talk about invitations that people have had to meet someone in a specific place – an invitation to attend an interview or a wedding; being asked to attend a surprise party.

Bible reading

Exodus 4:18–21 can easily be read by a narrator and three character voices. The people of Israel desperately needed someone to lead them. Moses was God's person. Moses was to care for these people even though it was to be very costly. A script from the CEV can be downloaded from **web ref AASA3.Sept_2**.

Bible retelling

This script, based on Acts 20:13–38, is suitable for a middle-aged actor (male or female) who is reminiscing about the past. Explain that they lived at the time of the apostle Paul.

The last time I saw the great apostle Paul must have been a good 20 years ago. He was travelling to Jerusalem for the festival of Pentecost, wanting to celebrate with some followers of the Way. He asked some of us Christians living in Ephesus to meet him at a port on the Aegean Sea. (Ephesus is a wonderful city, important for trade and for religious worship. It lies on the River Caÿster, which has got silted up so the city is no longer actually on the coast.)

Anyway, we went, of course. We love and admire Paul so much. He took the trouble to tell us, a bunch of Gentiles, what God was up to. He stayed here for three years until he was sure we understood. He never said it was going to be easy though – always told us how much it might cost to follow Jesus. And he showed us about Jesus by the way he lived. He never asked us for anything. He got out his canvases and started a tent-making business right here in the city. I don't know how he found time to make tents – he seemed to spend all his time talking to people about Jesus.

Anyway, we went to meet him on the coast. We were in for a big shock. He told us straight, 'You'll never see me again.' He said he expected to be put in jail, and worse. Everywhere he went, people who heard what God's Spirit was saying were telling him this message. We were devastated.

Then he gave us one last lesson in how to live. He reminded us how he'd been – gentle, loving, painfully honest. And he said, 'I'm not responsible for any of you. You have to be the shepherds now. You have to look after the flock of God's people.' None of us thought we could. But he reminded us that we had to trust that everything was in God's hands. He was our true Shepherd, even if we were doing the work!

It was so hard to say goodbye. I don't think we've ever prayed harder that the prophets might be wrong. And we cried and cried. But Paul was ready for whatever was coming, even if we weren't. And then he sailed away.

Bible talk

With: PowerPoint pictures of people or groups and the things or people they care for, eg doctors and patients, fans and football team, teacher and class, parents and children, zookeeper and animals, two helpers and someone in a wheelchair, grandparent and grandchild (available as a download from **web ref AASA3.Sept_1**); A4 sheets with the same pictures jumbled up, one sheet per person; pens or pencils to be used in groups

Ask the congregation to get into small groups to match up the images on the sheet into pairs. Give them a few minutes to do this and encourage them to identify why they have paired images up. Use the PowerPoint slides to show the correctly paired-up images and ask if anyone can identify what the common feature is for these pairs. Ask if any group had other ways of creating pairs and if so, what criteria did they use?

Confirm the suggestion, assuming it has been made, that these pairs are of those who care for other people, or animals or things. and the people or things they care for. In some cases, the care or love goes both ways. These examples help us begin to understand how Paul cared for the people in Ephesus and how they also cared for him. Fill in the detail for the benefit of those who do not know much about Paul's travels. If the children have already explored his journeys in their *Light* group, ask them to tell everyone what they have discovered.

In the same groups, ask people to identify either who cares for them or who they care for. How many examples of such care can they name? How many of these examples are two-way? Invite feedback from the groups.

Paul showed how much he cared by his determination to tell as many people as possible about Jesus.
This was personally very challenging and difficult for him. But he refused to be put off. Read Acts 20:18–21.

Paul cared so much about serving God that he wanted to finish whatever it was that God had set him to do.
He was prepared to obey God whatever it cost him. Read Acts 20:24.

Paul cared so much that he wanted to make sure that these followers of Jesus would be able to remain firm in their faith.
That was why he called them to come to see him as he travelled down the coast on his way to Jerusalem. He wanted them to know God loved them, and that they were in this together, serving God, sharing the good news and supporting each other. Read Acts 20:29–32.

Paul cared so much that he did not want to be a burden on these followers of Jesus.
He had always tried to be financially independent so that no one would feel burdened by his needs. Read Acts 20:33–35a. Comment on how much this is like a parent leaving their child at school for the first time, getting them prepared for what was facing them and not wanting to be a burden to their child.

Paul was convinced of how much God cares for his people. In Exodus, God planned to rescue his people from Egypt. He found just the right person – Moses – to rescue and lead them. Moses cared for the Israelites, but God cared even more, long before Moses began to care for them. Paul cared for the Ephesians, but God cared long before Paul arrived on the scene. We have people we care for,

but God cares for them far more than we do and he did this long before we began to care. We are all in it together – experiencing God's love and care and then sharing it with others.

Prayer activity
With: a large heart drawn onto a sheet of card; glue sticks; heart-shaped confetti

Ask everyone to be honest about whom they care for or love, and how they show it. Ask them to think about whether their care ever includes talking about Jesus and the difference he makes to our lives. As they call to mind these people who need to hear or be reminded about Jesus, ask them to say their names to God, asking him to bless them. Then ask them to stick some confetti on to the large heart to symbolise the place those people have in God's heart, and their own.

This prayer could be extended to include people already on God's heart whom we find hard to love.

Prayers of confession
With: print out the prayer below or project it on a screen – it can be downloaded from **web ref AASA3.Sept_3**

Heavenly Father,
We thank you that you love and care for us.
We thank you that we have heard and responded to the good news about Jesus.
But we have to tell you that we are not always good at sharing this good news.
We are sorry.
Give us your loving heart.
Help us to help others to see and know you.
Help us never to forget that you have called us to do this job together.
Amen

Ending the service
Paul knelt down with all the people who had come from Ephesus to meet with him and they prayed and cried and hugged each other. It would be appropriate, if possible, for everyone to kneel down and hold hands with those around them. (Be aware that elderly and infirm people may not be able to kneel to do this.) Each person should turn to the person on either side of them and say: 'I now place you in to God's care – today, tomorrow and until we next meet.' You may wish to display these words.

People can hug each other if appropriate. Remind them that they can be confident that, unless the Lord returns before you next meet, you are all likely to meet each other again, which was not the case for Paul and his friends. Encourage people this week to pray for those they have talked with during the course of the service.

Helpful extras

Game
Develop the theme of 'caring pairs', by asking teams to call out the 'partner' for a face put up on PowerPoint. This could include real-life husbands and wives in the congregation (or parents/children), cartoon buddies (eg Danger Mouse and Penfold), pairs from *Strictly Come Dancing*, and comedy duos like Laurel and Hardy.

Statement of faith
This is available as a download from **web ref AASA3.Sept_4**.

Notes and comments

If there are any children or young people starting a new school or course, or anyone about to begin a new job, make a point of praying for them in a commissioning sort of way, including their parents if appropriate.

The theme is particularly appropriate if this is a service when leaders of children and youth groups are being commissioned to serve God in the year ahead. Remind them that God has called them to this task, he will equip them, and they are not in this on their own but they are serving him together. Together they can support each other and nuture all those whom the 'Holy Spirit has placed in [their] care' (see Acts 20:28, CEV).

Great and small

Harvest-time

Aims: to recognise the stunning variety in the world that God has made
to join with all creation in praising God

Reading: Psalm 148:1–14

Getting started

An all-age harvest service often provides an opportunity for lots of participation for all ages, as well as being a time to welcome those who do not regularly attend a church service. If your church is in a rural setting, everyone will be aware of the traditional nature of a harvest festival. However, these days most people are aware of the environmental implications of food production and distribution, along with the nutritional values placed on what we eat.

This service moves beyond the understanding of harvest as simply a time to recognise the cycle of seasons and a time to be grateful for our food; instead, it guides everyone to marvel at the world that God has made. This will be done by acknowledging the sharp contrasts and opposites there are in creation, which should lead us to worship God. Psalm 148 does not contain many of these opposites but it does contain plenty of variety.

For the **Bible talk**, you will need imaginative access to Google Earth and other images of nature if the church is fitted with broadband. Alternatively, use a variety of images – for example, videos – of outer space and God's created world.

You will need:

- large and small sheets of paper plus pens for **Beginning the service**
- for the **Prayer activity**, squares of black card (8 x 8 cm), small sticky stars, crayons or chalk or glitter pens, silver thread at least 50 cm long
- For the **Game** download **web ref AASA3.Harv_1**
- For the **Statement of faith** download **web ref AASA3.Harv_2**
- for the **Bible talk** and **Prayers of intercession**, a variety of images of outer space and God's created world, see above

Beginning the service

With: very large sheets of paper and small ones, laid out on tables or the floor around the building; felt-tip pens

Invite everyone to draw something in God's created world that is very large on one of the large sheets of paper, and one thing that is very small on one of the small sheets. The large drawing does not have to cover the whole piece of paper because there needs to be room for other drawings. Some could be drawn inside the outline of others. Give suggestions such as an elephant, mountain and star or an ant, ground pepper and a wren.

Welcome everyone and introduce the theme. Show the drawings and comment on them; then sing a song that celebrates creation. During the singing of the song, everyone can bring their harvest gifts to the front, if that is your custom.

An additional or alternative 'gift' might be for people to bring to the front a picture or symbol (or the actual object) of something they like that God has made. Comment on these and then, together, sort them in various ways: great and small, hard and soft, local or far away, old or young, bright or dark, static or moving. You will need to advise people about this the week before and have some images or objects ready in case you do not get many examples brought to the front.

Bible reading

Present Psalm 148 with as many contrasts as possible. For example, using the CEV:
Verses 1 and 2 could be shouted out, while verses 3 and 4 could be whispered.
Verses 3 and 4 could be read from a high place, with verses 5 and 6 from ground level.
Verse 6 could be read slowly, with verse 7 read more quickly.
Verses 8–12 could have voices reading a word or phrase alternately, for example an old person and a young person. They could miss out the connecting words.
Everyone could join together to say 'Come, praise the LORD' in verses 7, 10 and 12.
Verses 13 and 14 could be read by two people from opposite sides of the building.

Comment on the variety in God's world and ask people if they have noticed how many contrasts there were in the reading.

Bible talk

With: pictures, downloaded images, or videos of outer space; if possible, see if you can display the church building (and any other building you wish to see) from space, and also explore outer space above the church

The vastness of creation is evidence of God's greatness

Everything in the sky above us, reaching far into outer space, is huge, although stars may look very small when viewed with the naked eye. Show the images of space to the most sophisticated degree you can access. If possible, look at images of the church building from space, commenting on any local landmarks, such as a school or a busy roundabout. Zoom in and out a couple of times to show people how small we are when seen from space.

Remind everyone what the writer in Psalm 148 called for in verses 1–4. Angels, sun, moon and stars were all to offer praise to God. The great God created all this vastness, and all of creation exists as evidence of God's greatness.

Tiny things in creation are evidence of God's greatness

But then, he created tiny creatures, made with such detail that the naked eye cannot see everything. Invite everyone to look at one of their forefingers. Can anyone count the number of lines on just the tip of their forefinger? How many different small movements can people do with their forefinger – forwards, backwards, sideways, curling up, crossing over? Allow 30 seconds for this, but some children might want a lot longer. The God who created this vast world also made it possible for us to make such tiny movements, with a finger that is made in such tiny detail.

The great God created all this variety, power and detail in creation; indeed, it is evidence of God's greatness. At this harvest-time, you are remembering God's goodness and detail in the provision of food that is grown, and not just in your own country! (At this point, you could zoom out to show the revolving earth to remind people of places around the world where food is grown.) Ask for suggestions – what grows in which country? Alternatively, show a globe and slowly revolve it.

Remind everyone that the writer in Psalm 148 also called on all creatures on earth to praise God (v 10).

The staggering variety in human beings makes us want to praise God

Devise a set of different pairs of descriptions that will demonstrate the variety of people that God has made. (These need to be physical characteristics or abilities rather than personal preferences – has God given someone the ability to support the local football team or to like their type of music or is that just a preference? You could discuss this - but it might be a distraction!)

This should be played as a game with people moving between two different designated places in the building. Alternatively, people can stand up to face one direction or the other, depending upon which description applies to them. For example: males go to the left side, females to the right; those with long hair or short hair; those who speak only English or another language as well; musical or not; fair hair or not; straight hair or wavy; over 18 or under 18.

Read out Psalm 148:11 and 12 again. Not only are our many differences evidence of the greatness of God's creation, but we can also praise God by how we live our lives and by what we say.

Conclude by singing a song that focuses on all of creation praising God such as, 'Let everything that has breath', 'Praise God from whom all blessings flow', or 'All creatures of our God and king'.

Prayer activity

With: squares of black card (8 x 8 cm) with one hole punched in a corner; small sticky stars; crayons or chalk or glitter pens that will write on the card; silver thread at least 50 cm long

Give everyone a card, pen and a star. A star should be placed in one corner of the card, which represents the night sky. The silver thread should be pushed through the hole and tied in a knot. A short phrase can be written on the card such as 'I will praise the Lord', or 'Thanks, God, for your huge world', or 'Thank you for stars'.

The card can be hung above a window at home as a reminder that God has made the vast world that we are part of.

When everyone has completed their card, invite them to stand in circles of up to six people. Each person speaks out their message of thanks to God; the leader then reads Psalm 148:13 in conclusion.

Alternatively, use this rhyme for young children.
I can hear and I can see.
(Cup ears and point to eyes.)

Thank you, God, for making me.
I am strong and I am free.
(Flex muscles and fling arms wide.)
Thank you, God, for making me.
You have made the earth and sea.
(Draw a circle in the air and then make waves.)
Thank you, God, for making me.
(Stretch up tall.)

Prayers of intercession

With: images of space, the earth and people, as in the **Bible talk**; alternatively, pictures of outer space, pictures of green fields and trees, pictures of people

Before the service, ask the young people to prepare the **Prayers of intercession** and any computer images to inform the prayers - outer space, plants, trees, and then human beings. Show the images on the screen (or hard copy).

Prayers could be as follows:
- Pray for all those who are exploring outer space, that they may acknowledge God's greatness.
- Pray for places in the world where there is a drought or deforestation, or where natural resources are damaged or in short supply. If you talked about places around the world where food is grown, you could make reference to these places.
- Pray for all those people who have got bored with life and have forgotten what an amazing world we live in. You should also pray for those who are to receive the harvest gifts.

Ending the service

Thank everyone for their gifts and for their participation. But most of all, you should end the service by thanking God. In the spirit of Psalm 148:14, invite everyone to shout out their thanks to God, by repeating the phrase they wrote on the card, as loudly as possible. If you did not include the **Prayer activity** in the service, ask everyone to think of one thing that they want to thank God for and then invite them to speak that out to God, as loudly as possible. Give them an example, such as 'Thank you, God, for your amazing world.' Conclude with a song of praise.

Helpful extras

Game

Display the word CREATION and ask the following questions. The letters in the answers are all in the word 'creation' and are all part of God's creation. They are also opposites. An electronic version of this game can be downloaded from **web ref AASA3.Harv_1**. To operate this, click the first slide to show the word CREATION. Read the first clue and when the correct answer has been given, click again and the answer will jump out of the word. The next click reverts to the word CREATION. This game could be used at any point in the service.

Water that falls from above (Rain)
Another name for a lake (Tarn)

A clean pet animal that purrs (Cat)
A dirty wild animal (Rat)

What exists above us (Air)
Metal found in the ground below us (Tin, iron)

A bird that flies above (Crane)
An insect that burrows underneath (Ant)

Something to suck to cool you down (Ice)
Something to drink to warm you up (Tea)

Statement of faith

This can be downloaded from **web ref AASA3. Harv_2**.

Notes and comments

The **Bible talk** makes use of Internet search engines, especially Google Earth, to demonstrate the vastness and the smallness of God's creation. This can also be used in the **Prayers of intercession**, especially if you are going to pray for places in the world where there is drought or deforestation.

This use of the Internet will capture people's attention but if you do not have appropriate Internet facilities or licensing agreements, you can create acetates or pictures of outer space and tiny created things to use instead. Note that videos need permission unless they are from a public domain source such as YouTube. Again downloaded images need to be from a public domain source or used with the permission of the website.

Make full use of the computer and creative skills of the congregation. The young people should be able to prepare any computer images needed to inform the **Prayers of intercession**.

For **Beginning the service**, plan how you will receive the harvest gifts (if at all) and distribute them. They do not have to be gifts of food that have been grown but could be toiletries and household goods, useful for those who are housebound or for a charity for the homeless

For the alternative **Beginning the service**, remember that the previous week you need to invite people to bring a representation of their favourite thing in creation (or the actual object). Another idea would be to ask people to bring in a matchbox the tiniest thing in creation that they can find. All contributions could receive a small prize. Decide which is the smallest or marvel at the variety of small things that people have brought.

All-age music and songs

For many people music and singing is a key element of worship and a great tool for communication with God. Here is an opportunity to learn doctrine and theology. If we are aiming for multi-sensory all-age worship, then music has a major part to play.

- **Music behind words.** Appropriate, non-intrusive background music playing behind prayers and confession, or during the talk, can help people focus on what is being said. If you weave a simple song in with responsive prayers, there is a cohesion and wholeness to that part of the service.

- **Music to teach.** The lyrics of songs, secular or spiritual, can bring out a teaching point as well as keeping all ages in touch with current musical cultural trends. Of course, to do this well, the church sound system needs to be able to cope. It is essential that the music is clear and the lyrics can be heard.

- **Music as a gift.** The ability to play a musical instrument is a skill and a gift from God. Church music groups vary greatly in style and quality, but however great (or otherwise) they sound, they are providing opportunities for people to develop their gifts. All-age worship should, ideally, be led by a music group of all ages, with experienced and learning adults alongside experienced and learning children and young people.

- **Music to set the atmosphere.** Playing a song or having a music group leading a few songs before the service formally begins brings people together. If you aim to begin the service with a time of thought and reflection, then quiet songs with a worship focus could be used. If you are aiming for a mood of celebration, more lively songs can be used. Last-minute arrivals can join in easily.

- **Song pitch.** Some new worship songs and many traditional hymns are pitched too high for most congregations. Take care in the choices of songs so that the congregation does not end up sounding like a cats' chorus on a bad day! Musically, a range of just over an octave, middle C to top D, will be possible for most children. Adults can usually manage a wider range. Teenage boys will struggle with pitch and singing for a whole lot of other reasons!

- **Song traditions.** Most all-age congregations will be looking for a range of songs to use in worship. Despite the yearning many of us have to be up to date and cutting edge, we are still part of a church whose traditions go back over 2,000 years. The first believers, meeting in secret, used spiritual songs and hymns in much the same way as David did hundreds of years before, and as we do today. While there is a place for 'said' services, there is also an important role for singing as an integral part of the whole.

- **Mixing it.** Always aim for a balance between songs that are more suited to young people and songs that are preferred by more traditional people. We do not want to alienate whole chunks of the worshipping community because we refuse to sing anything written before the Victorian hymns of the 1800s, or after the 'Seek Ye First' generation of the 1970s! A mix of different styles, a good range of songs and not overdoing songs avoids the worship feeling tired or repetitive.

- **Traditional hymns.** There is a place for traditional hymns in all-age worship. These are meaningful not only to older members of the congregation but may also be reassuring to people who go to church occasionally. Traditional hymns have a lot to teach us through their words. This is confirmed by the recent trend for contemporary worship songwriters to set traditional hymn words to new music. However, the hymns chosen need to be selected carefully, considering the tune, the words, the number of verses and the terms used in the lyrics. Miss out some verses, change a few words to make them more appropriate to modern culture, or talk through the meanings of some of the phrases before you begin.

- **Current worship styles.** Proceed with caution! There is a move towards songs that are very strongly led from the front and are therefore performed by the singers or worship leader. An ideal worship song would be one that everyone finds easy to learn and to sing, with clear ideas rather than abstract concepts. It is good to introduce new music, but always consider the ability of your musicians to deliver the song, the simplicity (or otherwise) of the melody and the relevance of the words.

- **Children's worship and praise.** Many children's songs are full of teaching and worship communicated in a lively way with appropriate words. But some songs patronise children with banal words! As a child, I learned much of my theology and many Bible verses through the songs I sang, songs which were modern for their day. We don't want children to have to unlearn something later in life that they thought was true, but wasn't!

- **Action songs.** It is a fundamental error to assume that children can only worship if there are actions involved! Action songs have their place and, if nothing else, adults can join in and call it occupational therapy! But children and young people are capable of worship without actions if they are led well and the songs chosen are understood.

- **Signing and singing.** Many schools now encourage all children including those who do not have communication difficulties to learn some basic sign language. This is a very powerful tool in all-age worship, as it is often suited to slower, more worshipful and reflective songs. Sign language gives physical focus for the words and helps people of all ages connect with the meaning. But remember – like everything else, it should be used sparingly and not overdone.

Think about…
Who has a say in the songs used in all-age worship?
How are the songs chosen, what range of books do they come from and who is consulted in the process?
Is it time to review the list of songs and reintroduce some golden oldies or bring in some fresh songs?

This has been taken from *Top Tips on All-age Worship* (SU) by Nick Harding and used with permission. This book is a short, easy to read book, which is full of invaluable advice for all of your all-age service team. It is available from all good Christian bookshops or Scripture Union Mail Order or online.

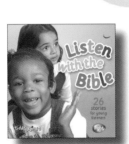

Listen with the Bible Story CD
978 1 84427 243 3
£9.99

Light for everyone music CD
978 1 84427 080 4
£14.99

Reach Up music CD
978 1 84427 169 6
£14.99

Bitesize Bible Songs music CD
978 1 84427 260 0
£9.99

Bitesize Bible Songs 2 music CD
978 1 84427 380 5
£9.99

These resources provide a wide range of songs, music, and *Learn and remember* verses in song form. Visit www.scriptureunion.org.uk/light to find out how you can download individual songs.

The Light Range...

light

Welcome to Scripture Union's family of *Light* resources.
There's a leader's guide, and children's and young people's materials for each age group, plus lots of extra resources to enhance your work with them. For more information visit **www.scriptureunion.org.uk/light**

5s and Under

5-8s

8-11s

11-14s

14-18s

All-age worship

Light for the Lectionary makes the approach and expertise of Scripture Union's market leading *Light* resources available to churches using a lectionary to explore and teach the Bible in their all-age worship services.

LightLive

LightLive is a new addition to the family of *Light* resources. Register free at **www.lightlive.org** today and discover an exciting approach to children's, youth and all-age ministry.